Step-by-Step

Build Your Perfect Workflow

Kiet Huynh

Table of Contents

Introduction

What is Asana?

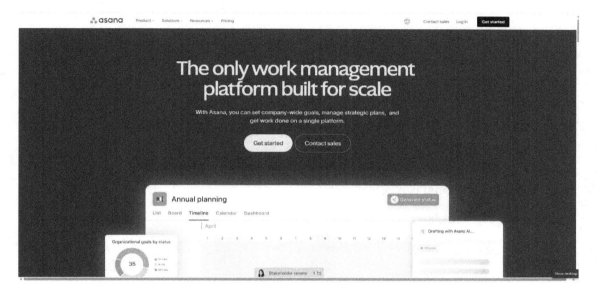

In today's fast-paced, interconnected world, managing work effectively is one of the biggest challenges faced by teams and individuals alike. Tasks pile up, deadlines creep closer, projects span across multiple departments, and communication often gets lost in a sea of emails and chat messages. Amidst all this chaos, having a structured system that keeps everything organized, transparent, and actionable becomes not just a luxury, but a necessity.

This is precisely where **Asana** comes in.

Asana is a powerful work management and collaboration platform designed to help individuals, teams, and organizations organize their tasks, streamline their workflows, and achieve their goals with clarity and efficiency. At its core, Asana provides a flexible digital workspace where work is easily captured, shared, tracked, and completed, all in one place.

But understanding Asana goes beyond simply knowing what it is—it involves appreciating its philosophy, its capabilities, and why it has become a vital tool for millions of users around the globe.

The Origin of Asana

Asana was founded in 2008 by **Dustin Moskovitz**, a co-founder of Facebook, and **Justin Rosenstein**, a former engineer and manager at Facebook and Google. Both had firsthand experience with the challenges of managing work across fast-growing teams. They realized that many teams spent more time coordinating work than actually doing it—a phenomenon they called "work about work."

The idea behind Asana was simple yet profound: **reduce "work about work"** and help teams spend more time on what truly matters—creative, strategic, and impactful work. The company's mission reflects this vision:

"Help humanity thrive by enabling the world's teams to work together effortlessly."

With that guiding principle, Asana was born—not just as another task manager, but as a comprehensive, adaptable platform to coordinate everything from small personal tasks to massive cross-functional projects.

What Asana Is—and Isn't

To understand Asana clearly, it's helpful to know what it is and what it is not.

Asana is:

- A **work management platform** for tracking tasks, projects, and workflows.

- A **collaboration tool** that helps teams communicate around work without relying solely on email or meetings.

- A **productivity enhancer**, offering features that make it easier to prioritize, plan, and execute work.

- A **customizable system** adaptable to various industries and teams, from marketing to product development, HR, finance, and beyond.

Asana is not:

- A traditional project management tool built solely for Gantt charts and resource allocation.

- A replacement for every communication tool (such as email or Slack).

- A rigid system requiring you to adapt to it; instead, Asana adapts to you.

This flexibility is part of what makes Asana so powerful: whether you are an individual freelancer managing multiple clients, a startup team launching a new product, or a multinational enterprise rolling out strategic initiatives, Asana can be molded to fit your needs.

Key Features and Functions

Before diving deep into how to use Asana, it's important to have a high-level overview of its main building blocks:

- **Tasks**: The fundamental units of work in Asana. Tasks can represent anything—an idea, a to-do, an assignment, or a deliverable.

- **Projects**: Groups of tasks organized around a shared goal or output. Projects help teams see all related work in one place.

- **Sections**: Dividers within projects that help organize tasks into different stages or categories.

- **Boards**: A Kanban-style view for visualizing tasks as cards across columns.

- **Calendar**: A timeline view that helps track when tasks are due.

- **Timeline**: A Gantt-chart-like feature for mapping out project schedules.

- **Portfolios**: Higher-level tracking of multiple projects across an organization.

- **Goals**: Tools for setting and measuring progress toward strategic objectives.

- **Automation**: Rules and triggers that automate repetitive processes.

- **Integrations**: Connections to other tools like Slack, Zoom, Google Drive, and more.

Understanding these core components will make it much easier to navigate Asana effectively.

Why Asana Matters in Modern Work Environments

In many workplaces today, project management isn't handled by project managers alone—it's a shared responsibility across every team member. Knowledge workers increasingly need autonomy, collaboration, and real-time visibility into the work that matters.

Asana addresses these needs by offering:

- **Clarity**: Everyone knows who is doing what and by when.

- **Accountability**: Tasks are assigned, deadlines are visible, and progress is transparent.

- **Efficiency**: Processes are streamlined, saving time otherwise lost to miscommunication or manual coordination.

- **Flexibility**: Different teams can work in ways that suit their styles, whether Agile sprints, Waterfall models, or simple to-do lists.

In remote and hybrid work settings especially, Asana becomes a digital headquarters where teams can align their efforts and stay connected without being physically together.

Who Uses Asana?

The beauty of Asana lies in its versatility. It is used by:

- **Individuals** managing personal productivity or side projects.

- **Small teams** coordinating marketing campaigns, design projects, product launches, etc.

- **Startups** tracking customer feedback, feature requests, and internal projects.

- **Large enterprises** managing complex, multi-department initiatives.

Organizations such as **Amazon, Google, NASA, Spotify,** and **Airbnb** have all used Asana to organize their operations, proving that it scales from the smallest teams to the largest global organizations.

Moreover, Asana fits diverse industries:

- **Marketing**: Campaign management, content calendars, event planning

- **Product Development**: Feature roadmaps, sprints, QA tracking

- **Operations**: Vendor management, internal processes, compliance tracking

- **HR**: Onboarding workflows, recruitment pipelines, employee engagement programs

- **Sales and Customer Success**: Deal tracking, client onboarding, support escalations

No matter your role or industry, Asana has a place in your daily workflow.

Asana's Evolution and Commitment to Innovation

Since its early days, Asana has consistently evolved. New features such as **Workload Management**, **Goals**, **Automation Rules**, and **Forms** have been added, responding directly to user needs.
Asana's leadership has remained focused on not just creating more features, but crafting a more coherent and intuitive system—making powerful work management accessible to everyone.

The company also emphasizes transparency and regular communication with users, offering annual updates, customer events like **Asana Together**, and partnerships with a network of Asana-certified experts worldwide.

This commitment to innovation ensures that learning Asana is not just investing in a tool, but adopting a dynamic platform that will continue to grow alongside you and your team.

Common Misconceptions About Asana

As you start using Asana, it's helpful to dispel a few common myths:

- **"Asana is too complex for small teams."** In fact, many small teams find Asana's simple task lists and boards perfect for lightweight work management.

- **"You need a project manager to use Asana effectively."** Not at all! Asana is designed to empower every team member to manage their own work easily.

- **"Asana is only for software development teams."** While developers can benefit greatly, marketing, operations, HR, and many other teams also thrive using Asana.

Clearing up these misconceptions early will help you approach Asana with the right mindset and confidence.

A Glimpse into What You'll Learn

In the coming chapters, you will embark on a step-by-step journey to:

- Set up your Asana workspace and projects.

- Create and assign tasks efficiently.

- Organize your projects for maximum clarity.

- Build custom workflows tailored to your needs.

- Collaborate seamlessly with your team.

- Integrate Asana with your favorite apps.

- Unlock advanced features for scaling your work.

Each chapter is designed to guide you not just in *using* Asana, but in mastering it—turning you into a confident, effective work manager regardless of your starting point.

By the end of this book, you will have the tools and knowledge to design your perfect workflow, boost your productivity, and make Asana a natural extension of how you work best.

Why Choose Asana for Work Management?

85% of Fortune 100 companies use Asana[4]

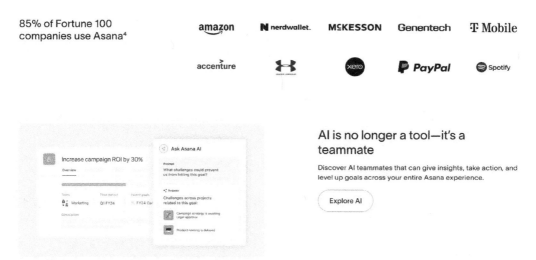

In today's dynamic, fast-paced work environment, teams are constantly striving to improve collaboration, streamline project management, and deliver results more efficiently. Traditional methods like endless email threads, spreadsheets, or scattered notes often create confusion rather than clarity. That's where Asana shines — offering a centralized, intuitive, and powerful platform designed specifically to simplify work management and empower teams to achieve their best outcomes.

Choosing Asana isn't just about adopting another tool; it's about embracing a smarter, more organized way of working. In this section, we'll explore why Asana has become the go-to solution for businesses, nonprofits, freelancers, and global corporations alike, and why it could be the perfect fit for your work management needs.

1. A Centralized Hub for All Your Work

One of Asana's most compelling strengths is its ability to centralize work. In a world where tasks, conversations, deadlines, and documents are often scattered across different systems, Asana serves as a single source of truth. Every project, every task, every update — all live in one place, easily accessible by everyone on the team.

No more digging through email chains to find the latest project update. No more losing track of deadlines written in someone's notebook. With Asana, your team operates from the same playbook, aligned and informed at every step.

Recognized as a leader by experts

2. Intuitive and User-Friendly Interface

Software adoption can be a hurdle for any team. A tool is only as good as the team's willingness and ability to use it. Asana excels with its clean, intuitive interface that feels natural even for first-time users.

You don't need to be a tech expert to create tasks, assign responsibilities, set deadlines, or track progress. Its drag-and-drop features, clear labeling, and customizable project views (List, Board, Calendar, Timeline) make it easy for users to visualize their work in the way that suits them best.

Learning curves are short — meaning teams can get up and running quickly, seeing value almost immediately.

3. Flexibility to Support Any Workflow

Every team is different. A marketing team might run campaigns, a product team might track feature launches, a sales team might manage customer pipelines. Asana's flexibility ensures that it's not a rigid system forcing teams into a single way of working. Instead, Asana molds itself around your needs.

You can customize task fields, project templates, tags, sections, and rules to mirror your team's unique workflows. Whether you're following Agile, Waterfall, Scrum, Kanban, or your own hybrid system, Asana adapts — not the other way around.

4. Powerful Project Visualization Options

Different people prefer different ways of seeing information. Some love the linearity of a list, while others prefer the flow of a Kanban board or the timeline of a Gantt chart. Asana offers multiple project views:

- **List View:** Perfect for detailed, itemized tracking.
- **Board View:** Ideal for visualizing stages in a workflow (like "To Do", "In Progress", "Done").
- **Calendar View:** Great for seeing tasks and deadlines over time.
- **Timeline View:** Essential for mapping out project dependencies and milestones.

Being able to switch seamlessly between these views ensures that every team member can manage their work in the way that suits them best.

5. Seamless Team Collaboration

Collaboration is more than just assigning tasks — it's about real-time updates, clear communication, and shared ownership. Asana enables this through features like:

- **Task Comments:** Collaborate directly within tasks.
- **Mentions:** Notify teammates when their attention is needed.
- **Attachments:** Share files directly in tasks.
- **Status Updates:** Keep everyone informed without needing lengthy meetings.

With Asana, you eliminate the silos and miscommunications that often plague teams, replacing them with transparency and accountability.

6. Automation to Save Time and Reduce Errors

Manual work slows teams down. Forgetting to assign a task, update a status, or move an item to the next stage are common human errors. Asana's **Automation** features — such as Rules, Triggers, and Integrations — allow you to automate repetitive tasks.

Imagine setting up a rule where every time a task is moved to "Review," it automatically notifies your Quality Assurance team. Or whenever a task is marked complete, a follow-up task is created automatically.

Automation ensures that processes are consistent, deadlines aren't missed, and teams stay focused on work that matters.

7. Comprehensive Progress Tracking and Reporting

One of the biggest challenges in managing projects is visibility. How do you know if you're on track? Are there bottlenecks forming? Are team members overloaded?

Asana's reporting tools — including **Project Dashboards, Milestones, Goals**, and **Workload** views — give managers and team members powerful insights without having to hunt for information.

You can quickly spot overdue tasks, see who's overloaded, track goal progress, and create beautiful visual reports to share with stakeholders.

8. Scalability for Teams of All Sizes

Whether you're a solo entrepreneur organizing your daily tasks or a multinational corporation managing complex, cross-functional initiatives, Asana scales with you. Asana offers solutions for:

- Individuals and small teams (Asana Personal and Basic)
- Growing businesses (Asana Premium and Business)
- Large enterprises with complex needs (Asana Enterprise)

With features like **Admin Console, Advanced Permissions, Security Controls,** and **Custom Integrations**, Asana meets the needs of both nimble startups and large corporations.

9. Extensive Integration Ecosystem

In the modern workplace, no tool works in isolation. Asana integrates with hundreds of popular apps, including:

- Communication tools (Slack, Microsoft Teams)

- File storage (Google Drive, Dropbox, OneDrive)

- CRM systems (Salesforce, HubSpot)

- Time tracking tools (Harvest, Everhour)

- Development tools (GitHub, Jira)

This ensures that Asana fits seamlessly into your existing tech stack, enhancing your workflows instead of disrupting them.

10. Commitment to Innovation and Improvement

The world of work is changing rapidly, and Asana is committed to staying ahead. With regular updates, new features, and a strong customer feedback loop, Asana continually evolves to meet the needs of modern teams.

Recent innovations like **Goals, Universal Reporting, Workflow Builder,** and **AI-Powered Features** show that Asana isn't content with standing still — it's pushing the boundaries of what work management software can do.

Conclusion: Why Asana Is a Game-Changer for Your Work

Choosing a work management platform is a strategic decision that impacts your team's day-to-day productivity, collaboration, and success. Asana offers more than just a task management tool — it provides a powerful, flexible, and scalable platform that aligns teams, clarifies priorities, automates processes, and delivers measurable results.

By choosing Asana, you're not just organizing tasks — you're empowering your team to work smarter, move faster, and achieve more.

Throughout this book, you'll learn how to unlock the full potential of Asana, build workflows that fit your needs perfectly, and transform the way you manage work forever.

Let's dive deeper and start building your perfect workflow with Asana!

How This Book Will Help You

In today's world, effective work management is not a luxury — it's a necessity. As businesses become more dynamic, teams more distributed, and projects more complex, the ability to organize tasks, prioritize goals, and collaborate seamlessly has become central to professional success. That's where Asana steps in — and that's where this book becomes your guide.

"Asana Step-by-Step: Build Your Perfect Workflow" is not just another user manual. It is a practical, hands-on roadmap designed to empower you to **master Asana's full potential**, regardless of whether you are a complete beginner, a casual user, or someone seeking to elevate your team's performance to the next level.

In this introduction, you'll discover exactly how this book will serve you, what you can expect to learn, and how to maximize the benefits of both Asana and this guide throughout your journey.

Comprehensive Learning, One Step at a Time

This book breaks down the complex world of Asana into clear, digestible steps. Rather than overwhelming you with dense technical jargon or assuming prior experience, we start from the basics and build gradually toward advanced usage.

You will learn:

- How to set up your Asana account and navigate the platform confidently.

- How to create and organize projects and tasks efficiently.

- How to customize workflows to match your unique working style or organizational needs.

- How to automate repetitive processes to save time and minimize human error.

- How to collaborate effectively with teammates and stakeholders.

- How to integrate Asana with other tools you already use.

Each chapter and section is purposefully structured to equip you with both **conceptual understanding** and **practical skills** you can apply immediately.

Built for All Users — Individuals, Teams, and Organizations

Whether you are managing your personal projects, leading a small team, coordinating cross-functional enterprise initiatives, or setting up an entire project management office, Asana can adapt — and so can this book.

You'll find tips, examples, and best practices tailored for different users:

- **Solo professionals and freelancers** can learn how to use Asana as a personal productivity system.

- **Team leaders and project managers** will discover strategies for organizing team efforts, assigning responsibilities, and tracking progress.

- **Business owners and executives** will uncover ways to use Asana's higher-level features like Portfolios and Goals to align strategy with execution.

Hands-On Exercises and Practical Examples

Theory is valuable, but practice is where true mastery happens. Throughout the book, you will find:

- **Hands-on exercises**: Step-by-step activities to reinforce each major lesson.

- **Real-world examples**: Sample projects like marketing campaigns, product launches, client onboarding, and event planning to see Asana in action.

- **Common pitfalls**: Lessons on what mistakes to avoid when implementing Asana in your workflow.

By actually using Asana as you read, you will develop the confidence and muscle memory needed to manage real work without hesitation.

Workflow First, Tools Second

MAXIMIZE IMPACT

Automate workflows across departments

It's easy to get caught up in learning every feature a software tool offers, but tools are only effective when they serve a **clear workflow**.

This book teaches you how to design your own workflows first, then use Asana to bring those workflows to life.

You will learn how to:

- Visualize your work processes.

- Break work down into manageable tasks.

- Choose the right project structure (Board vs. List, etc.).

- Automate routine steps intelligently.

- Monitor performance and continuously improve.

By following this workflow-first approach, you won't just be learning Asana — you'll be learning **how to design smarter ways to work**.

Tailored to Modern Work Environments

Remote work, hybrid teams, asynchronous communication, multi-project juggling — modern work environments present unique challenges. This book addresses those challenges directly, showing how Asana can be your **central**

hub for clarity, communication, and collaboration, no matter where your team members are located or how varied your project portfolio is.

We'll cover features like:

- Centralized team communication.

- Project visibility and transparency.

- Integrations with communication tools like Slack and Zoom.

- Notifications management to avoid overwhelm.

- Mobile app usage for work on the go.

You'll learn how Asana can **keep everyone aligned** — without endless meetings and email chains.

Stay Current with Asana's Evolution

Technology evolves, and so does Asana. Throughout the book, you'll find guidance on:

- Staying updated with new feature releases.

- Adjusting your workflows as Asana introduces improvements.

- Using community resources like Asana Academy and Asana's official forums.

You'll gain not just the skills to use today's Asana, but the mindset and flexibility to continue adapting as the tool evolves.

Focused on Real Results, Not Just Features

Many guides focus on features. This book focuses on **outcomes**.

The real question is not "Do you know how to create a task?" The real question is "Can you create a system that ensures every important task gets completed on time with minimal stress?"

Throughout this book, you'll be encouraged to focus on:

- Delivering projects efficiently.

- Reducing stress and burnout.

- Building systems that scale as your responsibilities grow.

- Enhancing personal and team accountability.

- Increasing visibility and transparency across your organization.

In short, this book is about **building results-driven workflows**, not just learning a tool.

Accessible Language, Professional Insights

You don't need to be a tech wizard to read this book. The language is straightforward, the steps are clearly laid out, and every technical explanation is paired with a real-world context.

At the same time, the insights are drawn from **professional project management, productivity best practices, and years of real-world Asana use** — ensuring you not only learn how to do things, but **why** certain practices are more effective than others.

Who Should Read This Book

This book is designed for:

- New users of Asana looking for a comprehensive and friendly starting point.

- Occasional users who want to unlock more of Asana's potential.

- Team leads, project managers, and department heads searching for ways to manage collaboration more efficiently.

- Entrepreneurs and small business owners building systems for growth.

- Anyone responsible for getting things done — better, faster, and with less stress.

No matter your background, if you want to take control of your projects and workflows with Asana, this book is for you.

How to Get the Most Out of This Book

Here are some tips to maximize your learning:

1. **Follow Along Actively**: Set up your Asana account (if you haven't already) and follow the exercises in real time.

2. **Apply Lessons Immediately**: Use your own projects as test cases while learning new features and techniques.

3. **Don't Skip the Exercises**: They are designed to reinforce the lessons and help you retain skills.

4. **Customize As You Go**: Adapt the examples and workflows to suit your own needs and style.

5. **Stay Curious**: Explore features beyond what's covered if they seem useful for your specific context.

Remember: mastery is built through **practice, experimentation, and reflection**.

A Final Word Before We Begin

You are about to unlock a new level of clarity, control, and confidence in your work.

Imagine feeling fully on top of your tasks, your projects progressing smoothly, your team collaborating effortlessly, and your goals being met consistently. That is the power of mastering Asana — and that is the journey we are about to embark on together.

Let's dive in and start building your **perfect workflow**!

CHAPTER I
Getting Started with Asana

1.1 Setting Up Your Account

1.1.1 Creating an Asana Account

If you are ready to transform the way you organize your work, collaborate with teams, and manage projects, your journey begins with creating an Asana account. This seemingly small first step opens the door to a world of structured productivity and seamless teamwork.

In this section, we will walk through every detail of the account creation process — from signing up for the first time to setting basic preferences that will shape your experience.

Why You Need an Asana Account

Asana is a cloud-based platform, meaning that all your data, tasks, projects, and workflows are stored online and accessible from any device. An account is necessary not just to log in but to personalize your workspace, integrate with your team, and gain access to advanced features like custom fields, project templates, and workflow automations.

An Asana account serves as your personal dashboard in a vast ecosystem. It enables you to:

- **Create and manage tasks** for yourself and your teams
- **Track project timelines and deadlines**
- **Collaborate and communicate** with colleagues
- **Integrate** with other productivity tools like Slack, Google Drive, Zoom, and more
- **Visualize work** in multiple views like list, board, calendar, and timeline

Now, let's get into the step-by-step process of creating your Asana account.

Step 1: Choosing Your Sign-Up Method

Asana offers several flexible ways to create an account, catering to your convenience. You can sign up using:

- **Email Address**
- **Google Account**
- **Microsoft Account**
- **Apple ID** (for Mac users)

Depending on your existing ecosystem (for example, if your organization uses Google Workspace), signing up with an existing account can save time and simplify integration later on.

Tip: If you plan to use Asana professionally or with a team, it is highly recommended to sign up with your work email address.

Step 2: Visiting the Asana Website

Go to www.asana.com. On the homepage, you will see a prominent button that says **"Get Started"** or **"Try for Free"**. Click it to begin the sign-up process.

Alternatively, you can go directly to the sign-up page via https://asana.com/signup.

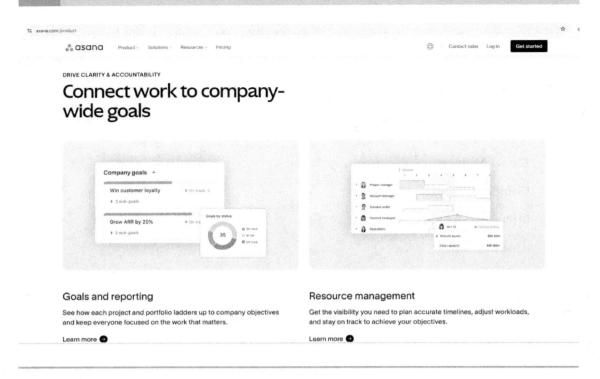

Step 3: Entering Your Information

If you choose to sign up using an **email address**, the site will ask for:

- Your email address

- Your full name

- A password

Asana encourages the use of strong, secure passwords, so consider using a combination of uppercase and lowercase letters, numbers, and symbols.

If you sign up with **Google**, **Microsoft**, or **Apple ID**, the platform will request permission to access basic account information like your name and email address for authentication.

Note: No sensitive personal information is collected without your consent.

Step 4: Email Verification

After submitting your information, Asana will send you a verification email to confirm your identity.

Open your inbox, locate the email from Asana (check your spam/junk folder if you don't see it within a few minutes), and click on the **"Verify Email Address"** button inside.

Verification is crucial because it:

- Ensures that you own the email address you provided

- Activates your account

- Secures your workspace

Step 5: Setting Up Your Profile

Once you verify your email, you will be redirected back to Asana, where you can:

- **Upload a profile picture** (optional but highly recommended for collaboration)

- **Set your display name**

- **Adjust your notification preferences** (email updates, mobile alerts, etc.)

Having a completed profile helps your teammates easily identify you and enhances communication across projects.

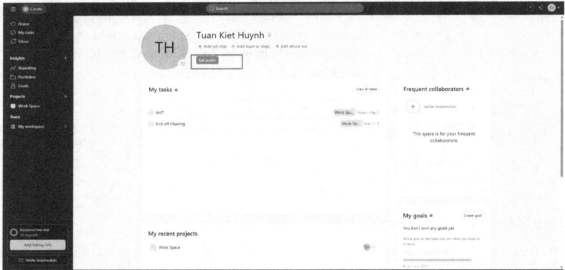

Step 6: Choosing a Work Environment

After setting up your profile, Asana will guide you through setting up your work environment:

- **Joining an existing team or organization:** If your email domain (like @companyname.com) matches an existing Asana organization, you may be prompted to join automatically.

- **Creating a new team or organization:** If no matching organization exists, you can start your own. This will serve as the workspace where you manage projects, invite collaborators, and structure tasks.

You'll also have the option to choose:

- **Personal use:** If you're using Asana to manage personal tasks or freelance work

- **Team use:** If you're collaborating within an organization or business team

Tip: If you're not sure, you can always adjust these settings later.

Step 7: Choosing a Plan (Free or Paid)

Asana offers several pricing tiers:

- **Basic (Free):** Ideal for individuals or small teams getting started

- **Premium:** Adds features like timelines, advanced search, milestones, and forms

- **Business:** Unlocks portfolios, workload management, and advanced integrations

- **Enterprise:** Tailored for large organizations needing extensive administrative controls and security

During setup, Asana may offer you a free trial of Premium or Business for a limited time. You can opt to accept the trial or stick with the free Basic plan.

Recommendation: If you're new to Asana, start with the free version. Once you're familiar with the basics, you can evaluate whether you need premium features.

Step 8: Setting Initial Preferences

Before diving into projects, you can set some basic preferences, such as:

- **Default start page:** Choose whether you want to land on My Tasks, a specific Project, or the Inbox when you log in.

- **Notification preferences:** Decide how and when you want to be notified about task updates, mentions, and project changes.

- **Time zone:** Ensure deadlines and due dates reflect your correct local time.

These minor details can drastically improve your initial user experience.

Common Challenges and Troubleshooting

While the sign-up process is usually smooth, here are common issues and solutions:

- **Didn't receive the verification email?** Check your spam folder or click "Resend Email" on the Asana sign-up page.

- **Can't sign up with a work domain?** Your company may have restricted Asana access. Contact your IT department for help.

- **Signed up but can't access certain features?** You might be using the Basic (free) plan. Consider upgrading or asking your team admin to add you to a paid workspace.

Best Practices for Account Setup

- **Use your real name and photo** to enhance trust and communication with team members.

- **Secure your account** by setting up two-factor authentication (2FA) once you log in.

- **Understand workspace vs. organization:** A **workspace** is great for individuals and small teams without a shared domain. An **organization** is structured around company email domains and supports multiple teams.

Summary: Your Gateway to Asana

Creating an Asana account is quick but essential. It not only grants you access to one of the most powerful project management tools available but also sets the foundation for how you interact with your work, your team, and your goals.

By carefully setting up your profile, workspace, and preferences, you lay the groundwork for a smooth and successful Asana experience.

Now that your account is ready, it's time to take your first step into the Asana world: **navigating the interface.**

Let's move forward to the next section: **Navigating the Asana Interface**.

1.1.2 Navigating the Asana Interface

When you first log in to Asana, it's natural to feel both excited and slightly overwhelmed. Asana's power lies in its robust yet intuitive interface that allows users to manage projects of any complexity. In this section, we will guide you step-by-step through understanding the Asana interface so you can start working confidently and efficiently.

The First Look: The Asana Dashboard

Once you successfully log in, you are greeted by the Asana Dashboard. This is your mission control — a central place where you can see an overview of all your workspaces, teams, and most recently accessed projects.

The dashboard includes:

- **Home**: A customizable overview of your important tasks and projects.

- **My Tasks**: A view listing all tasks assigned to you across different projects.

- **Inbox**: Notifications about activity that is relevant to you.

- **Reporting**: Analytics and insights across your projects.

- **Portfolios** (for premium users): An overview of high-level initiatives.

- **Goals** (for business users): Set and track strategic goals.

Understanding where each major feature lives is the first step in mastering the platform.

Breaking Down the Main Interface

Let's explore the primary components of the Asana interface in more detail:

1. Sidebar

The sidebar is located on the left-hand side of the screen and acts as your main navigation menu. Key elements include:

• **Home**: Access your customized overview.

• **My Tasks**: See all tasks assigned to you, organized by due date or priority.

• **Inbox**: Review updates on tasks and projects you are involved with.

• **Teams**: Access projects organized under various teams.

• **Projects**: Open specific projects to view or edit tasks.

• **Portfolios** and **Goals**: Track broader work initiatives.

You can collapse or expand the sidebar by clicking the three-line menu icon at the top, which is helpful if you want a cleaner workspace view.

Tip: Pin your most-used projects or teams to the sidebar for quick access.

2. Top Bar

The top bar is essential for quick actions and navigation. Here, you will find:

- **Quick Add Button (+)**: Quickly add new tasks, projects, messages, or goals.

- **Search Bar**: Search across tasks, projects, conversations, and even attachments.

- **Profile Settings**: Access your settings, notification preferences, and log out.

- **Help and Resources**: Get assistance directly from Asana's support or explore tutorials.

The top bar ensures that no matter where you are inside Asana, you are always just one click away from important actions and settings.

3. Main Pane (Project or Task View)

When you select a project or task, the middle section of your screen becomes the Main Pane. This is where you spend most of your time in Asana:

- **Project View**:

  o **List View**: Tasks organized in a checklist.

  o **Board View**: A Kanban-style board for visual project management.

  o **Calendar View**: Tasks plotted on a calendar based on due dates.

  o **Timeline View**: A Gantt-style view for understanding project dependencies.

- **Task View**:

  o **Task Title**: A short, descriptive name for the task.

  o **Assignee and Due Date**: Assign who is responsible and when it's due.

  o **Description**: Add detailed information, checklists, and bullet points.

  o **Attachments**: Upload files directly to tasks.

  o **Comments**: Collaborate with teammates directly in the task.

  o **Subtasks**: Break the task into smaller parts.

Each view has its own benefits depending on your workflow needs.

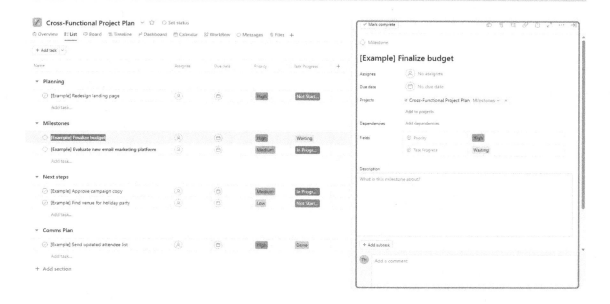

4. Task Details Pane (Right Pane)

Clicking on a specific task opens the Task Details Pane on the right-hand side. It gives you complete information about the selected task:

- **Edit the task title**
- **Add subtasks**
- **Change the assignee or due date**
- **Attach files and links**
- **Comment for collaboration**
- **View task history**

Having a dedicated pane for task details helps you stay focused on the task without navigating away from the broader project view.

Navigating Between Views

One of Asana's greatest strengths is allowing users to switch between multiple views easily. At the top of any project page, you will see view options:

- **List**
- **Board**
- **Calendar**
- **Timeline**

You can flip between them effortlessly depending on the type of project you're working on.

Example:

- Managing a content calendar? Use the **Calendar View**.
- Running an agile software development sprint? **Board View** with columns like "To Do," "In Progress," and "Done" will fit better.

Customizing Your Workspace

Asana allows a surprising level of customization to help tailor the workspace to your needs:

- **Sort Tasks**: By due date, project, or priority.
- **Filter Tasks**: See only tasks assigned to you, due soon, or marked high-priority.
- **Favorite Projects**: Keep your most important projects easily accessible.
- **Adjust Notification Settings**: Choose how and when you want to be alerted.

Spending a little time personalizing your Asana experience early on will pay off with much greater productivity down the line.

Understanding Asana Icons and Buttons

Here are some key icons you will encounter:

Icon/Button Meaning

📋   Create new task

Icon/Button Meaning

Create new project

Quick Add (task, project, goal)

Search bar

Settings and preferences

Notifications

Home dashboard

Recognizing these icons at a glance makes your navigation experience faster and smoother.

Keyboard Shortcuts for Faster Navigation

Asana supports many keyboard shortcuts to speed up your work. Some favorites:

- **Tab + Q**: Quickly add a task.
- **Tab + A**: Assign a task.
- **Tab + D**: Set a due date.
- **Tab + X**: Mark a task complete.

You can view the complete list of shortcuts by pressing **Tab + /** on your keyboard.

Mobile and Desktop Applications

Asana is available beyond your web browser:

- **Mobile Apps**: iOS and Android versions offer a streamlined experience for managing tasks on the go.
- **Desktop App**: A distraction-free dedicated Asana app is available for both Windows and MacOS.

Navigating between the web, desktop, and mobile versions is seamless — your changes sync instantly.

Common Navigation Mistakes to Avoid

Even though Asana's interface is user-friendly, new users sometimes stumble. Here are some common mistakes:

- **Ignoring the Sidebar**: Forgetting that many powerful navigation tools live there.

- **Overlooking Notifications**: Missing updates that could cause task delays.

- **Not Using Views Strategically**: Sticking only to the List View when a different view might better suit the project.

- **Too Many or Too Few Projects**: Poor project organization leading to confusion.

Being aware of these can help you avoid frustrations early.

Summary

Navigating Asana might feel a little daunting at first, but once you get comfortable with the dashboard, sidebar, project views, and task details, you will find it a powerful ally in work management.
By mastering the layout and functionality of the interface, you position yourself for greater efficiency, better collaboration, and ultimately smoother workflows.

In the next section, we will dive deeper into **Setting Up Your First Project** to put your new navigation skills into practice!

1.1.3 Understanding Asana Terminology

When you first step into the world of Asana, it can feel like learning a new language. Like any powerful platform, Asana uses specific terminology to describe its features, functions, and ways of working. Understanding these core terms is crucial because they form the foundation of how you will organize, manage, and collaborate on your projects inside

Asana. In this section, we will walk you through the key Asana terms, explain what they mean, how they fit together, and offer examples to make everything crystal clear.

Let's dive into the essential Asana terminology you need to know:

Task

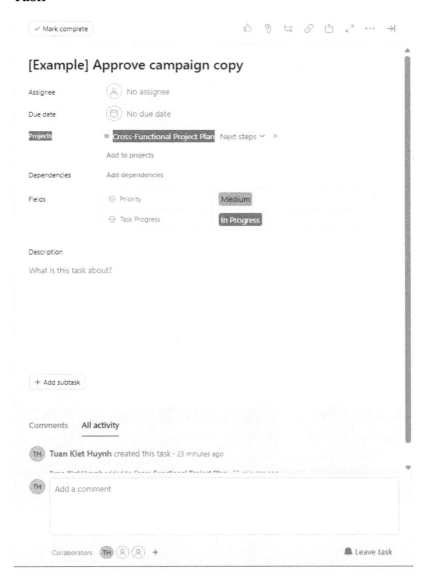

At the heart of Asana is the **task**. A task is a single unit of work that needs to be completed. Tasks can be big or small—ranging from "Create a marketing plan" to "Email client about meeting schedule." Every task can have:

- A name
- A description
- A due date
- An assignee (person responsible for completing it)
- Attachments
- Subtasks
- Comments

Example:

Task: "Design homepage banner"

- Assignee: Anna
- Due Date: Friday
- Description: Create a promotional banner for the product launch.

Tasks are the building blocks of all work in Asana. You will spend a significant amount of time creating, updating, and completing tasks.

Subtask

Subtasks are tasks nested inside a larger parent task. They help you break down complex tasks into smaller, manageable pieces. Each subtask can have its own assignee and due date, independent of its parent task.

Example:

Parent Task: "Plan Product Launch Event" Subtasks:

- Book venue
- Hire caterer

- Send invites

Using subtasks wisely helps you avoid overwhelming yourself or your team with a massive to-do list inside one task.

Project

Projects are containers for tasks. A **project** is where you group related tasks together in one organized space. Projects can be:

- Simple to-do lists

- Sophisticated workflows

- Major initiatives with hundreds of tasks

Projects allow you to visualize work in multiple formats like **List view**, **Board view** (Kanban style), **Calendar view**, or **Timeline view**.

Example:

Project: "Website Redesign" Tasks within the project: "Update homepage", "Revise about page", "Improve SEO".

In a project, you can manage deadlines, track progress, and collaborate with others.

Section / Column

Sections (in List view) or Columns (in Board view) are ways to organize tasks within a project.

- In **List view**, sections are headers you use to group tasks.

- In **Board view**, columns are used to represent stages of a process (like "To Do", "In Progress", "Done").

Example:

Section: "Phase 1: Research" Tasks under this section: "Interview users", "Analyze competitor sites".

Sections and columns make it easier to structure your projects logically and visually.

Assignee

The **assignee** is the person responsible for completing a task or subtask. Only one person can be assigned to a task at a time, ensuring accountability.

Example:

Task: "Write blog post" Assignee: John Doe

Clear task ownership prevents confusion and delays.

Due Date

A **due date** is the date by which a task should be completed. You can set due dates on tasks and subtasks to keep work on schedule.

Example:

Task: "Submit quarterly report" Due Date: October 15

Due dates create a timeline for your team and help prioritize work.

Milestone

A **milestone** represents a significant checkpoint or achievement within a project. Milestones help track major progress points and keep the team motivated.

Example:

Milestone: "Website ready for beta testing"

Milestones often don't require action themselves but mark important dates.

Timeline

Timeline is a visual way to see how tasks overlap and how long each task will take. Think of it like a Gantt chart. Timeline view helps you plan and adjust project schedules.

Example:

Seeing that "User Testing" must finish before "Launch" can begin.

Using Timeline, you can drag tasks to adjust their start and end dates easily.

Dashboard

The **Dashboard** offers a high-level overview of project status through charts and widgets. You can track how many tasks are completed, overdue, or in progress at a glance.

Example:

A pie chart showing that 70% of tasks are completed, 20% are overdue, and 10% are in progress.

Dashboards are perfect for managers who need quick insights without digging into details.

Workspace / Organization

- A **Workspace** is a shared space where users can collaborate on projects and tasks.
- An **Organization** is a workspace tied to a company domain (like @yourcompany.com) and provides additional administrative controls.

If you're working solo or with freelancers, you might use a simple Workspace. If you're working within a company, you're probably in an Organization.

Example:

Workspace: "Freelance Projects" Organization: "Acme Corp"

Team

A **Team** is a group of people working together on one or more projects inside an Organization.
Each team has its own projects and conversations.

Example:

Team: "Marketing Department" Projects under the team: "Campaign Management", "Content Calendar"

Teams help keep projects and communications organized around departments or focus areas.

Conversation

Conversations allow you to communicate directly within Asana, either within a project or a team. You can post announcements, ask questions, or discuss project-wide updates.

Example:

Conversation Topic: "Ideas for Q4 marketing campaigns"

Conversations reduce the need for endless email chains and keep discussions centralized.

Task Dependency

Dependencies allow you to set one task as dependent on another. A task can't be started until the task it depends on is completed.

Example:

Task A: "Design logo"

Task B: "Publish website" (dependent on Task A)

Dependencies help manage workflow sequences and avoid bottlenecks.

Rule

Rules are automation tools that help reduce manual work by automatically triggering actions based on specific conditions.

Example:

Rule: "When a task is moved to 'Done', mark it complete."

Rules allow you to automate repetitive processes inside your workflows.

Form

Forms allow people inside or outside your team to submit requests or information that automatically create tasks in a project.

Example:

Form: "Submit IT support request"

Forms are useful for structured work intake without cluttering your communication channels.

Portfolio

A **Portfolio** is a collection of multiple projects that you want to track together. It's especially helpful for managers overseeing multiple initiatives at once.

Example:

Portfolio: "2025 Strategic Initiatives"

Projects inside: "Launch new product", "Expand to Europe", "Hire key executives"

With Portfolios, you gain a bird's-eye view of your organization's progress.

Goal

Goals help you set, track, and align objectives across your team or organization. They are high-level targets connected to measurable outcomes.

Example:

Goal: "Increase website traffic by 25% in Q3"

Linking tasks and projects to goals ensures everyone's efforts are contributing toward larger strategic objectives.

Conclusion: Mastering Asana Language

By familiarizing yourself with Asana's core terminology, you're laying the foundation for successful navigation and usage of the platform. Each term represents a fundamental concept that ties into how Asana organizes and manages work.

Think of these terms like building blocks—you'll be using them constantly as you create tasks, set up projects, collaborate with teammates, and automate workflows.

In the next section, we'll walk through setting up your **first project**, where you'll put this knowledge into action and see how these elements come together in real-world use.

Ready to build your first Asana project? Let's move on!

1.2 Setting Up Your First Project

1.2.1 Choosing the Right Project Template

Starting a new project in Asana is an exciting step toward better organization and team collaboration. Before you dive into adding tasks and deadlines, it's essential to start on the right foot—by choosing the project template that best fits your workflow and goals. Asana offers a wide variety of pre-built templates designed to save you time, provide structure, and help you visualize your project from the beginning.

In this section, we'll walk through the importance of templates, how to choose the right one for your needs, and offer practical advice on customizing a template for maximum impact.

Why Templates Matter

A project template acts as a framework, offering a predefined structure with sections, tasks, and sometimes timelines already laid out for you. Instead of building everything from scratch, a template helps you:

- **Save time:** Quickly get started without creating every task and section manually.

- **Ensure consistency:** Especially helpful if you manage multiple projects with similar formats.

- **Visualize progress faster:** Immediate structure makes it easier for your team to understand their responsibilities.

- **Avoid missing key steps:** Templates often include best practices and key milestones relevant to the project type.

Whether you are planning a marketing campaign, managing a product launch, or onboarding new employees, the right template can dramatically improve efficiency and clarity.

Exploring Asana's Template Library

Asana's built-in Template Library offers dozens of options across various departments and use cases. Some of the main categories include:

- **Marketing:** Campaign management, content calendars, event planning

- **Product Management:** Roadmaps, feature launches, sprint planning

- **Design:** Creative requests, design production workflows

- **Human Resources:** Employee onboarding, recruitment pipelines

- **Sales and CRM:** Sales pipelines, account tracking

- **Operations:** Vendor management, inventory tracking

- **IT:** Bug tracking, IT project management

Each template is crafted based on industry best practices, making it a reliable starting point for most common business processes.

To access templates in Asana:

1. Click the **+** button next to "Project" in the sidebar.

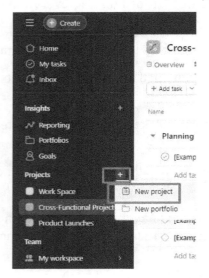

2. Select **Use a Template** from the options.

Create a new project
How would you like to start?

3. Browse templates by category or search using keywords.

4. Preview templates to see the layout and included tasks.

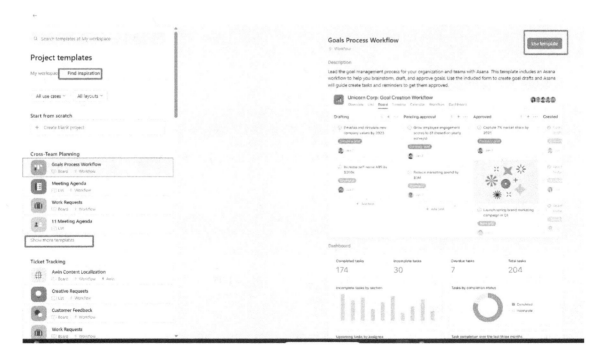

Factors to Consider When Choosing a Template

Not every template will fit your specific needs right out of the box. Here's what you should consider when picking the right one:

1. Project Type and Scope

Ask yourself:

- Is this a simple, one-off project?

- Is it a recurring process that should be standardized?

- Is it complex and multi-phased, requiring detailed stages?

For example, a **Marketing Campaign** template is great for a multi-channel product launch, whereas a **Simple Project Plan** is better for smaller, short-term tasks.

2. Team Size and Collaboration Needs

Some templates are better suited for large cross-functional teams (e.g., company-wide events), while others are optimized for small teams or even individuals.

Templates designed for larger teams may include more detailed task breakdowns, handoffs, and review processes.

3. Timeline Sensitivity

If your project is highly deadline-driven (e.g., software release dates), choose a template that already incorporates milestones and Gantt chart (Timeline) views.

Asana's **Product Launch** or **Event Planning** templates, for instance, focus heavily on timing.

4. Reporting Requirements

If your stakeholders require frequent updates or progress reports, templates that include milestones and dashboards make it easier to visualize and communicate progress.

Some templates integrate reporting sections or dashboards by default.

5. Customization Potential

Consider how easily you can modify the template. You may need to:

- Add/remove tasks

- Rename sections

- Adjust task owners and deadlines

- Add custom fields specific to your industry

Pick templates that allow flexibility without needing a complete overhaul.

Popular Asana Templates: A Closer Look

Here's a quick overview of some of Asana's most widely used templates:

Template Name	Best For	Key Features
Simple Project Plan	Small teams, solo projects	Task lists, minimal setup
Marketing Campaign	Marketing teams	Channels, asset creation, deadlines
Employee Onboarding	HR teams	Pre-built checklists, documents, first-week tasks
Bug Tracking	IT support, development	Prioritization fields, assignment tracking
Content Calendar	Marketing, editorial teams	Schedule views, publishing deadlines
Sprint Planning	Product development teams	Iteration cycles, backlog management

Each template comes with predefined tasks, and most include example content that you can edit or delete based on your specific needs.

Custom Templates: When to Create Your Own

Sometimes, the available templates won't perfectly match your project's requirements. Asana allows you to create **Custom Templates** based on your projects.

You might want to create your own template if:

- You frequently manage similar types of projects.

- Your organization has a unique workflow that generic templates don't cover.

- You want a branded or process-specific project framework.

To create a custom template:

1. Create a new project and set up the structure you want.

2. Click on the project's title and select **Save as Template**.

3. Name your template, add a description, and categorize it appropriately.

From there, anyone on your team can duplicate the template when starting a new project.

Best Practices for Choosing and Using Templates

Here are several actionable tips:

- **Preview before committing:** Always click through a template to make sure it fits your real-world workflow.

- **Simplify where possible:** Start with fewer sections and tasks; add complexity only as needed.

- **Communicate with your team:** Involve key stakeholders in the selection process if multiple teams are collaborating.

- **Document your customizations:** Keep a written record of any major changes you make to a template so future team members understand the structure.

- **Review templates periodically:** As your workflows evolve, your templates should too. Schedule a regular review every 6–12 months.

Common Mistakes to Avoid

- **Choosing a template that's too complex:** More isn't always better. Overly complex templates can overwhelm new users.

- **Ignoring customization:** Using templates without adjusting them to fit your workflow can cause confusion.

- **Skipping training:** If your team is new to Asana, provide a brief orientation session to explain how the template works.

- **Neglecting mobile considerations:** If team members primarily work from mobile devices, ensure the template structure is mobile-friendly.

Checklist: Choosing the Right Template

Use this checklist to ensure you're making the right choice:

- Does the template fit my project type and scope?

- Is it suitable for my team size and collaboration needs?

- Are the timeline and milestones relevant?

- Can I easily customize the template?

- Does it include necessary reporting tools?

- Is it aligned with how my team prefers to work?

If you answer "no" to any of these questions, keep browsing or consider building your own template.

Conclusion: Laying a Strong Foundation

Choosing the right project template is not just a technical step—it's a strategic one. A thoughtfully selected template sets clear expectations, fosters better communication, and keeps the entire team aligned on deliverables. By investing time upfront to select or design the right template, you dramatically increase the odds of your project's success.

In the next section, we'll move forward with **Creating Projects from Scratch**, giving you the flexibility to tailor every detail of your workflow when a template just won't cut it.

1.2.2 Creating Projects from Scratch

Creating a project from scratch in Asana is a fundamental skill that empowers you to fully customize your work environment to meet the specific needs of your team or personal workflow. Unlike using pre-made templates, building your project from the ground up offers unparalleled flexibility and control. In this section, we'll walk through the entire process—from the initial setup to tips for structuring your project effectively.

Why Create a Project from Scratch?

Before diving into the how-to, it's important to understand why you might choose to create a project from scratch rather than using a template:

- **Complete Customization**: You decide every detail—structure, sections, tasks, fields—tailored precisely to your unique workflow.

- **Flexibility**: You are not constrained by pre-defined settings that might not fit your project type or team's style.

- **Skill Building**: Creating projects from scratch helps deepen your understanding of Asana's powerful features and options.

- **Scalability**: You design the project with future scaling in mind, allowing for more seamless growth.

Step-by-Step: Creating a New Project from Scratch

Let's explore how you can build a project from the ground up.

Step 1: Navigate to the Project Creation Area

- From the main sidebar in Asana, locate the **"Projects"** section.

- Click the **"+ New Project"** button.

- You will be presented with two main options:

    o **Use a Template**

    o **Blank Project (Start from Scratch)**

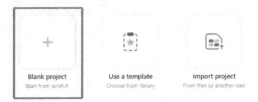

Select **"Blank Project"** to begin creating from scratch.

Step 2: Name Your Project and Choose Its Basics

New project

Project name

Privacy

👥 My workspace ⌄

✦ Set up with Asana AI

Continue

Once you select "Blank Project," Asana will prompt you to input essential project details:

- **Project Name**: Choose a clear, descriptive name that captures the project's purpose. (e.g., "Marketing Campaign Q4", "Product Launch Plan", "Team Onboarding Process")

- **Team Assignment**: Decide which team (if any) the project belongs to. You can create private projects or share them within a team.

- **Privacy Settings**: Choose between:
  - **Public to Team**: Anyone in the team can access.
  - **Private to Project Members**: Only invited members can see the project.

- **Project Layout**: Select how you want to visualize your project:
  - **List** (task-oriented, linear format)
  - **Board** (Kanban-style, ideal for stages and workflows)
  - **Timeline** (for Gantt-chart style planning, available with paid plans)
  - **Calendar** (date-driven overview of tasks)

Select the layout that best matches how you visualize the work.

Step 3: Create Sections or Columns

After setting up the basics, your project will open in the chosen view.

- **List View**: Click **"Add Section"** to create headers for task grouping.

- **Board View**: Each column represents a stage in your workflow (e.g., To Do, In Progress, Completed).

Sections or columns help break down the project into manageable phases, categories, or milestones.

Pro Tip: Use sections to mirror phases of a process, like "Planning," "Execution," and "Review," or to categorize by functional area like "Design," "Development," and "Marketing."

Step 4: Add Tasks and Subtasks

With your sections set, start adding individual tasks:

- **Click "Add Task"** within a section.

- **Task Title**: Keep it action-oriented. (e.g., "Draft blog post", "Design logo concepts")

- **Details**: You can add a detailed description, attach files, set priority, add tags, and more.

- **Subtasks**: Click into any task and create subtasks for detailed steps or checklists related to the parent task.

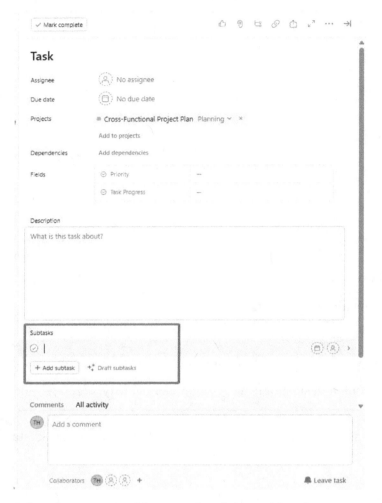

Subtasks are crucial for complex deliverables that require multiple steps to complete.

Step 5: Set Due Dates, Assignees, and Priorities

Each task should be actionable:

- **Assignee**: Assign tasks to team members or yourself.

- **Due Date**: Establish deadlines to keep the project on track.

- **Priority Tags**: You can use custom fields or tags to indicate priority levels (e.g., High, Medium, Low).

Setting ownership and timelines ensures accountability and progress.

Step 6: Add Custom Fields (Optional but Powerful)

Custom fields allow you to track additional important information, such as:

- Task status (e.g., Not Started, In Progress, Completed)
- Budget
- Project phase

- Approval needed

You can create drop-downs, numbers, text fields, and more to tailor your project tracking.

Best Practices for Designing Projects from Scratch

Now that you know the basic mechanics, let's elevate your projects to a professional level.

1. Keep It Simple at First

Avoid overcomplicating your first projects. A clean, simple structure with clear phases and tasks will be more effective than an overly elaborate one.

2. Consistent Naming Conventions

Develop a standard way of naming tasks, sections, and projects across your organization for clarity and consistency. Examples:

- Tasks: **[Department] - [Action] - [Deliverable]**
- Sections: **[Phase] - [Goal]**

3. Color Coding and Icons

Use color coding or emojis in section names to visually distinguish different parts of your project.
Example:

- 🚀 Launch Preparation
- 📣 Marketing Rollout
- 🛠 Development Phase

4. Use Templates for Recurring Projects

Once you've created a solid project structure from scratch, save it as a **template** for future use. This can dramatically speed up future project creation.

5. Review and Optimize Regularly

No project structure is perfect from the start. Build in regular reviews to tweak and optimize sections, custom fields, or workflows based on team feedback and evolving needs.

Common Mistakes to Avoid When Creating Projects

- **Overloading One Section**: Spread tasks logically across multiple sections to avoid a bottleneck.

- **Neglecting Due Dates**: Tasks without deadlines tend to get overlooked.

- **No Clear Ownership**: Always assign every task to someone responsible.

- **Ignoring Customization**: Leverage custom fields and views; don't stick with default settings if they don't serve your project needs.

Real-World Examples of Projects Created from Scratch

Example 1: Product Launch

- **Sections**:
  - Research & Development
  - Marketing Strategy
  - Launch Execution
  - Post-Launch Analysis
- **Custom Fields**: Priority, Budget, Approval Status
- **Views**: Board View for agile visual management

Example 2: Team Onboarding

- **Sections**:
  - Week 1: Introduction
  - Week 2: Core Training
  - Week 3: Shadowing & Mentoring
- **Tasks**: IT setup, HR documentation, Orientation meetings
- **Views**: List View for checklist-style tracking

Example 3: Content Calendar

- **Sections**:
  - Content Ideas
  - In Progress
  - Scheduled
  - Published
- **Tasks**: Blog posts, social media campaigns, email newsletters
- **Views**: Calendar View for date-centric planning

Summary: The Power of Building from Scratch

Creating a project from scratch in Asana might feel intimidating at first, but it offers ultimate control over how you work. By starting with a blank slate, you can tailor the project structure to perfectly match your team's needs, processes, and goals.

Remember:

- Think about your team's real needs before setting up the structure.
- Don't be afraid to start simple and evolve your project as you go.
- Consistency, clear ownership, and deadlines are your best friends.

Mastering this foundational skill sets the stage for building more complex workflows, collaborating effectively, and scaling your productivity in Asana. In the next sections, we'll dive deeper into how to organize, automate, and supercharge your projects for long-term success.

1.2.3 Inviting Team Members

Introduction: Why Team Collaboration Matters in Asana

One of the greatest strengths of Asana lies in its ability to enhance team collaboration. Projects are rarely solo efforts—whether you are managing a marketing campaign, a product launch, or internal operations, involving the right people at the right time is crucial for   success.

Inviting team members into your Asana project enables you to distribute work efficiently, maintain transparency, improve accountability, and foster seamless communication. In this section, we will explore why inviting team members early is important, how to invite them correctly, permissions and roles you can assign, and best practices for setting up a collaborative environment.

1. Understanding the Importance of Team Invitations

Before you start clicking the "Invite" button, it is important to understand the strategic reason behind inviting team members.

- **Shared Ownership**: When teammates are added early, they feel a sense of ownership over the project's success.

- **Transparency**: Everyone knows what is happening, reducing confusion and miscommunication.

- **Efficient Work Distribution**: Tasks can be assigned directly to responsible individuals, which streamlines accountability.

- **Enhanced Productivity**: Collaborative planning saves time, ensures milestones are hit, and minimizes bottlenecks.

A project with the right people involved from the start has a much higher chance of success.

2. Preparing Before You Invite

Before sending out invitations, a little preparation goes a long way:

- **Define Roles**: Know who will be responsible for what. Will Sarah lead content creation? Will John oversee timelines?

- **Set Expectations**: Decide what access level each person should have (editor, commenter, viewer).

- **Organize Structure**: Make sure your project's Sections, Tasks, and Milestones are outlined. You don't need everything finalized, but a basic skeleton helps new members understand the context quickly.

3. How to Invite Team Members to Your Project

Step-by-Step: Inviting Teammates

1. **Open Your Project** Navigate to the project where you want to invite people.

2. **Locate the Share Button** In the top-right corner of the project window, you'll find the "Share" or "Invite" button (it often looks like a person icon with a plus sign).

3. **Enter Email Addresses or Names** If your team members already have Asana accounts within your organization, you can simply start typing their names. If they are new to Asana, you can invite them via their email addresses.

4. **Assign Roles/Permissions** Choose the appropriate permission level for each invitee:

   o **Editor**: Can modify tasks, projects, and settings.

   o **Commenter**: Can comment but cannot make structural changes.

   o **Viewer**: Can only view content.

5. **Send the Invitation** Once you've selected the right people and assigned the correct roles, click "Invite." Your team members will receive an email notification or an in-app alert if they already have an account.

4. Understanding Permissions and Access Levels

Permissions in Asana are critical for maintaining control over sensitive information and ensuring appropriate collaboration. Here's a closer look:

Role	Capabilities
Editor	Create, modify, assign, and delete tasks; edit project settings.
Commenter	View and comment on tasks, but no editing or deletion allowed.
Viewer	Only view content; cannot comment, edit, or delete.

Choosing the right permission helps avoid accidental deletion or miscommunication. For highly sensitive projects (e.g., strategic planning, product launches), limit editing rights to only a few core members.

---

5. Managing Team Member Notifications

When you invite someone to a project, Asana automatically sends notifications. While this is useful, it can become overwhelming if not managed well.

Here's how to manage this:

- **Notification Settings**: Encourage team members to customize their notifications (via Asana settings) to avoid inbox overload.

- **Status Updates**: Use project status updates strategically so people receive summarized, meaningful information instead of scattered task alerts.

Pro Tip: You can tag specific team members in the comments of tasks to draw their attention without bombarding the entire team.

---

6. Adding Guests and External Collaborators

Sometimes, your project might require collaboration with people outside your organization—freelancers, clients, or consultants. In Asana, you can invite **Guests**. Here's what you need to know:

- **Guests** are users who join via a different email domain than your organization's.

- They have limited access: only to the specific projects and tasks they are invited to.

- Guests cannot browse your organization's entire workspace.

Inviting a Guest:

- Enter their external email address (e.g., consultant@gmail.com) into the Invite field.

- Set appropriate permissions, usually Commenter or limited Editor rights.

This keeps sensitive information within your team while still allowing necessary collaboration with outsiders.

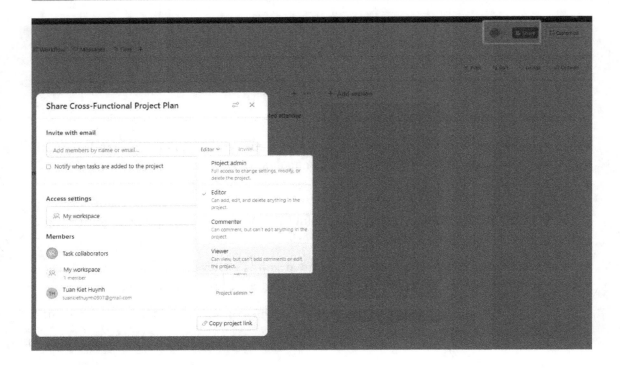

7. Best Practices for Team Onboarding in Asana

To ensure your team members are productive as soon as they join the project, consider these best practices:

Create a Welcome Task or Section

Create a special "Welcome" task or section that includes:

- Project overview
- Key objectives
- Important deadlines
- Links to resources (Google Docs, SharePoint, Dropbox folders)

Assign First Tasks Immediately

Assign a small, introductory task to each new team member so they quickly become active in the project.

Provide a Quick Training

Offer a 15-30 minute walkthrough (live or recorded) showing how your team uses Asana:

- Naming conventions for tasks
- Workflow rules
- Expectations for updates and comments

Encourage Questions

Create a "Questions" section or task where team members can post any queries about the project.

8. Troubleshooting Common Invitation Issues

Sometimes, you might run into minor issues when inviting team members:

Problem	Solution
Invitation not received	Ask them to check spam/junk folder; resend invitation.
Wrong email address	Double-check the spelling or domain name.
Access denied	Ensure your organization's Asana admin settings allow external invites if needed.
User can't see project	Verify they were invited to the correct project and permission level is set properly.

If problems persist, contacting Asana Support or your organization's Asana Admin can help resolve them.

9. Advanced Tip: Using Teams and Portfolios for Larger Groups

If you're working on a large initiative involving multiple projects and dozens of people:

- **Create a Team in Asana** (group of people organized around a function or project).
- **Use Portfolios** to group multiple projects together for easier overview and management.
- You can invite people at the **Team Level**, giving them access to all team projects.

This is particularly useful for department-wide projects or cross-functional collaborations.

Conclusion: Building the Foundation for Project Success

Inviting the right team members and setting them up for success is the foundation of effective project management in Asana. By taking the time to plan invitations strategically, manage permissions carefully, and onboard your team thoughtfully, you set your project up for smooth collaboration, clear communication, and outstanding results.

Remember:
A project is only as strong as the team behind it. And with Asana's powerful collaboration features, your team has everything it needs to thrive.

1.3 Exploring the Asana Workspace

1.3.1 Sidebar Overview

When you first log into Asana, one of the most immediately noticeable elements is the **Sidebar**. Think of the Sidebar as the **navigation control center** for your entire Asana workspace. It offers quick access to all the major areas where your projects, tasks, teams, and organizational structures live. Mastering the Sidebar is essential for a smooth and productive experience.

In this section, we will take a **deep dive** into each part of the Sidebar, how it functions, what you can customize, and best practices for using it to streamline your workflow.

Understanding the Sidebar Layout

The Sidebar typically appears on the left-hand side of your screen and remains visible unless you choose to minimize it for a more focused view. It's organized into **several key sections**, each designed to help you move effortlessly between different components of Asana.

The main elements of the Sidebar include:

- **Home**
- **My Tasks**
- **Inbox**
- **Reporting**
- **Teams and Projects**
- **Portfolios (Premium feature)**
- **Goals (Premium feature)**
- **Saved Searches and Favorites**

Let's walk through each of these elements carefully.

Home: Your Starting Point

The **Home** button at the top of the Sidebar brings you to a personalized dashboard. Here, you will find:

- **Upcoming Tasks** based on deadlines.

- **Project Highlights** from your active workspaces.

- **Recommendations** such as suggested tasks to focus on.

- **Announcements** from Asana.

Best Practices for Home:

- Use the Home view each morning to quickly assess your priorities.

- Customize widgets if available to match your working style.

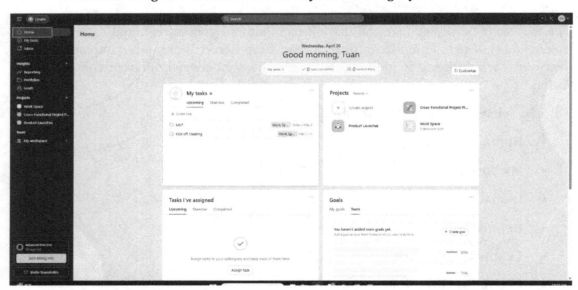

My Tasks: Your Personal To-Do List

My Tasks is where all the tasks assigned to you live. It's effectively your **personal command center** within Asana. Tasks here are typically organized by due date, and you can customize how they are grouped and viewed.

Key sections within My Tasks:

- **Recently Assigned**: New tasks you haven't organized yet.

- **Today**: Tasks due today.

- **Upcoming**: Tasks due soon.

- **Later**: Tasks due later or without an imminent due date.

Tips for Managing My Tasks:

- Check this view daily to prioritize your workload.

- Use keyboard shortcuts (Tab+Y, Tab+U, Tab+L) to quickly move tasks between Today, Upcoming, and Later.

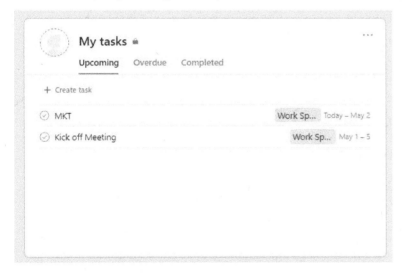

Inbox: Your Communication Hub

The **Inbox** is your **notification center**. Here, you'll find:

- Updates on tasks you're following.

- Comments on tasks you're assigned to.

- Project changes.

- Status updates.

You can **filter** notifications based on their importance and archive them after reading.

Inbox Best Practices:

- Regularly clear out your Inbox to stay informed without feeling overwhelmed.

- Customize notification settings to avoid unnecessary distractions.

Reporting: Visualizing Work Progress

Asana's **Reporting** tab gives you the ability to:

- Track the number of tasks completed.

- Monitor workload across teams.

- Create custom charts and dashboards.

This feature is especially powerful for team leaders or project managers who need a **quick snapshot** of productivity.

Common Reporting Uses:

- Spotting bottlenecks in workflows.

- Understanding individual team member outputs.

- Providing visual data for leadership reports.

Teams and Projects: Organizing Your Workspaces

Below the core navigation items, you'll see a list of your **Teams** and their associated **Projects**.

- **Teams**: Groups of people collaborating on related projects. Teams can be organized by department (e.g., Marketing, Development, HR).

- **Projects**: Individual initiatives or deliverables tracked inside a team.

You can **expand** and **collapse** Teams in the Sidebar to view the projects within them.

Project organization tips:

- Pin most-used projects to the top for quick access.

- Archive completed projects to keep your Sidebar clean.

Portfolios (Premium Feature)

If you are using Asana Premium, Business, or Enterprise, you'll also see **Portfolios**. A Portfolio is a **collection of projects**, giving you a bird's-eye view of their progress in real time.

Portfolios are ideal for:

- Managing multiple related projects.

- Tracking overarching company initiatives.

- Providing updates to executives.

Portfolio Tips:

- Use color coding to distinguish different types of projects.

- Add custom fields like project owner, deadline, or health status.

Goals (Premium Feature)

Also available in premium plans, **Goals** allow you to **align project work with organizational objectives**.

In the Sidebar, Goals help you:

- Set high-level outcomes.

- Connect goals to specific tasks and projects.

- Monitor progress toward strategic initiatives.

Using Goals Effectively:

- Set measurable and time-bound goals.

- Link goals to specific projects to ensure alignment.

Saved Searches and Favorites

At the bottom of the Sidebar, you'll find areas where you can:

- Save common **search queries**.

- Mark projects, tasks, or reports as **Favorites**.

These tools are extremely helpful for:

- Quick navigation.

- Reducing repetitive searching.

- Keeping important information readily available.

Best Practices for Favorites:

- Favorite your daily working projects.

- Update your Favorites list monthly to reflect current priorities.

Customizing the Sidebar

You're not stuck with a static Sidebar! Asana lets you customize it to better fit your workflow.

You can:

- **Drag and drop** Teams and Projects to reorder them.

- **Collapse Teams** you don't need immediate access to.

- **Hide** or **show** different sections depending on your preferences.

Additionally, Asana automatically **reorders projects** in the Sidebar based on recency of access if you don't manually pin them.

Customization Tips:

- Group similar projects together for faster switching.

- Pin the three to five projects you use most frequently.

Sidebar Navigation Shortcuts

To maximize efficiency, consider memorizing a few handy shortcuts:

- **Tab + H**: Go to Home.

- **Tab + Q**: Go to My Tasks.

- **Tab + I**: Open Inbox.

- **Tab + R**: Open Reporting.

Knowing these shortcuts can save precious time throughout the day.

Common Mistakes to Avoid

1. **Cluttered Sidebar**: Too many unarchived projects can make the Sidebar overwhelming. Archive finished projects to maintain a clean workspace.

2. **Ignoring Notifications**: Letting Inbox pile up can cause missed updates. Manage notifications daily.

3. **Not Using Favorites**: Favorites drastically cut down navigation time. Use them liberally for smoother work.

4. **Underutilizing Reporting**: Many users don't take full advantage of Reporting features. Learn to build simple dashboards for better team visibility.

Summary: Mastering the Sidebar

The Sidebar may seem simple at first glance, but it's a **powerful navigation and organization tool** at the core of your Asana experience. By understanding each section, customizing your view, and using best practices, you can move through Asana intuitively and maintain high levels of productivity.

Remember:
A well-managed Sidebar = a well-managed Asana workflow = a well-managed work life.

1.3.2 My Tasks, Inbox, and Reporting

When you first log into Asana, the core experience you'll interact with revolves around three primary areas: **My Tasks**, **Inbox**, and **Reporting**. These components serve as the control center for organizing, tracking, and responding to your work. Understanding and mastering these features is crucial for using Asana effectively, whether you're an individual contributor or managing a large team.

In this section, we will explore each of these tools in depth, with practical examples and tips for maximizing their impact on your daily workflow.

Understanding My Tasks

My Tasks is your personal to-do list inside Asana. It automatically collects all tasks assigned to you across all your projects and workspaces, providing a centralized view of your responsibilities.

Key Features of My Tasks

- **Automatic Aggregation**: Every task assigned to you appears in your My Tasks, eliminating the need to manually gather tasks from different projects.

- **Customizable Organization**: You can sort tasks by due date, project, priority, or custom fields.

- **Multiple Views**: Asana offers List, Board, and Calendar views for My Tasks, allowing you to choose the format that fits your workflow.

Using Sections in My Tasks

Sections help you break down tasks into manageable categories. By default, Asana offers sorting by:

- **Recently Assigned**
- **Today**
- **Upcoming**
- **Later**

You can also create custom sections, such as:

- "High Priority"
- "Waiting for Input"
- "Client Deadlines"

This allows you to fully personalize how you approach your daily planning.

Task Management in My Tasks

From the My Tasks view, you can:

- **Create new tasks** directly.
- **Mark tasks complete** with a simple click.
- **Reschedule tasks** by dragging them to new dates in the Calendar view.
- **Add subtasks** if a task requires multiple steps.
- **Attach files and notes** for richer task context.

Tips for Managing My Tasks Effectively

- **Review My Tasks daily** to ensure you don't miss deadlines.
- **Use color-coded tags or custom fields** for better visual organization.
- **Prioritize tasks at the start of your week** to stay focused.

Pro Tip: You can automate task sorting in My Tasks using *Rules* (e.g., move tasks with an upcoming due date into the "Today" section automatically).

Exploring Inbox

The **Inbox** in Asana is where you receive updates about the projects and tasks you're involved in. Think of it as your real-time notification center.

What Appears in the Inbox?

- **Task Updates**: Changes to tasks you're assigned to or following.

- **Project Changes**: When a project you're a member of has significant updates.

- **Mentions**: When someone @mentions you in a comment.

- **Status Updates**: New project status reports.

You can **filter your Inbox** to show:

- All updates

- Only updates on tasks you are assigned to

- Only mentions

Actions You Can Take in Inbox

From the Inbox, you can:

- **Mark notifications as read or unread**.

- **Archive notifications** once you've reviewed them.

- **Jump directly to the task or project** linked to the notification.

- **Comment or like** updates without leaving the Inbox.

Best Practices for Using Inbox

- **Clear your Inbox daily** to stay on top of changes.

- **Mute updates** from projects that are less relevant to reduce noise.

- **Respond quickly to mentions** to keep workflows moving smoothly.

Pro Tip: Use the mobile app to check your Inbox on the go and stay connected with your team even when away from your computer.

Understanding Reporting in Asana

Reporting gives you a bird's-eye view of the progress across projects, tasks, and teams. With Asana's built-in reporting tools, you can measure productivity, identify bottlenecks, and keep stakeholders informed.

Types of Reports in Asana

1. **Basic Reporting (Dashboard Widgets)**

   o Available for each project.

   o Offers simple visualizations such as pie charts, bar graphs, and status summaries.

2. **Advanced Reporting (Universal Reporting)**

   o Combines data across multiple projects.

   o Allows you to create custom charts based on specific criteria (e.g., overdue tasks by team, tasks completed this month).

3. **Workload Reporting**

   o Visualizes how much work is assigned to each team member.

   o Helps managers balance workloads and avoid burnout.

Key Metrics to Track

- **Task Completion Rates**: Track how many tasks are completed versus pending.

- **Due Date Performance**: Monitor how often deadlines are met or missed.

- **Milestone Achievement**: See the progress towards key project goals.

- **Resource Allocation**: Evaluate who has too many or too few tasks.

Creating Custom Reports

You can build custom reports based on:

- Project

- Assignee

- Tags

- Custom Fields (e.g., Priority, Department)

You can also save and share reports with your team to keep everyone aligned.

How to Access Reporting

- **Project Dashboards**: Inside any project, click "Dashboard" to view project-specific reports.

- **Reporting Tab**: On the main navigation bar, click "Reporting" to create cross-project dashboards.

Integrating My Tasks, Inbox, and Reporting for Maximum Productivity

While each tool is powerful on its own, the real magic happens when you use them together:

- Start your day by **reviewing your Inbox** for urgent updates.

- Move to **My Tasks** to organize and plan your day.

- End the week by **checking Reporting dashboards** to evaluate progress and plan next steps.

This cyclical approach ensures you're always acting on the most critical work, managing your time effectively, and keeping your team projects on track.

Common Pitfalls and How to Avoid Them

Pitfall	How to Avoid
Letting My Tasks become cluttered	Regularly review and clean up old tasks
Ignoring Inbox notifications	Set a daily routine to check Inbox

Pitfall	How to Avoid
Misinterpreting Reporting data	Customize reports carefully with clear filters

Quick Tips Summary

- **Pin critical projects** to easily find them from your sidebar.

- **Use shortcuts** like Tab+M to quickly assign tasks to yourself.

- **Set up Rules** in My Tasks to automate sorting and priorities.

- **Customize Inbox settings** to reduce unnecessary notifications.

- **Schedule regular report reviews** for continuous improvement.

By mastering **My Tasks**, **Inbox**, and **Reporting**, you build a foundation for a disciplined and efficient workflow that empowers you and your team to achieve more with less stress.

In the next section, we will explore how to **Create and Assign Tasks** effectively to get your projects moving forward with clarity and speed.

Ready to move from understanding your workspace to actively managing tasks? Let's dive into Chapter 2: Managing Tasks and Projects!

CHAPTER II
Managing Tasks and Projects

In Asana, tasks are the foundation of every project. Each task represents a single unit of work that needs to be completed, whether it's writing a blog post, preparing a report, scheduling a meeting, or designing a product feature. Managing tasks efficiently is crucial for personal productivity and team collaboration. This chapter will dive deep into creating, organizing, and assigning tasks and projects to streamline your work.

2.1 Creating and Assigning Tasks

Creating tasks and assigning them correctly is the first step toward building a strong project management system inside Asana. The task structure is flexible enough to suit both simple to-do lists and complex project workflows.

Before we delve into the details, let's understand **why** task creation and assignment are so critical:

- It clarifies ownership.
- It ensures visibility for deadlines and priorities.
- It enables better collaboration across teams.

In the sections below, we will go step-by-step through adding tasks, creating subtasks, and using Asana's features to make your task management more effective.

2.1.1 Adding Tasks and Subtasks

What is a Task in Asana?

A **task** in Asana represents an action item. It can stand alone or be part of a larger project. Each task can have its own details: assignee, due date, description, attachments, and comments.

Asana tasks can be:

- Standalone tasks (independent)

- Part of a project

- Grouped within sections or columns

- Connected with other tasks through dependencies

Tasks keep the team organized and provide a central location for all work-related discussions, documents, and updates.

How to Add a Task

There are multiple ways to create a task in Asana, depending on your workflow and preferences:

Method 1: Adding a Task from "My Tasks"

1. **Navigate to "My Tasks"** on the sidebar.

2. **Click the "+ Add Task" button** or press the keyboard shortcut **Tab + Q**.

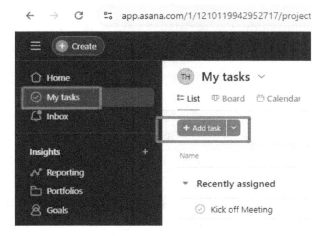

3. **Enter the Task Name** – this is the main title.

4. **Press Enter** to create the task.

5. After creation, click on the task to:

   o   Assign it to yourself or someone else.

   o   Set a due date.

   o   Add a description or attachments.

Method 2: Adding a Task Within a Project

1. **Open a Project** where you want to create the task.

2. If using the **List View**, click **"Add Task"** at the top or in the appropriate section.

3. If using the **Board View**, click **"+ Add Task"** within a column.

4. Follow the same steps: enter the task title, then click to add more details.

Method 3: Quick Add Button

1. Click the **Quick Add (+)** button usually located at the top bar of Asana.

2. Select "Task."

3. Fill in the task details: project, assignee, due date, and description.

Keyboard Shortcuts for Faster Task Creation

- **Tab + Q**: Open Quick Add Task anywhere in Asana.

- **Tab + N**: Create a task within a project.

Using shortcuts greatly improves speed for heavy users.

Best Practices When Adding a Task

- **Be specific with task names.** Instead of "Meeting," use "Client Onboarding Meeting – Prepare Agenda."

- **Set clear deadlines.** Always assign a due date to avoid forgotten tasks.

- **Assign ownership immediately.** A task with no assignee can easily fall through the cracks.

- **Use descriptions wisely.** Add context, links, and brief instructions.

Example of a well-structured task:

- **Title**: "Draft Product Launch Email"

- **Description**: "Draft the initial email for product launch. Include key features, call-to-action, and launch date."

- **Assignee**: John Doe

- **Due Date**: May 15

- **Attachments**: Link to product images

Understanding Subtasks

While tasks are primary units, **subtasks** help break down tasks into smaller, manageable pieces.

When to Use Subtasks:

- When a task is complex and needs internal steps.
- When multiple team members need to contribute to one task.
- When you want to create a mini-checklist within a task.

Example: Main Task: "Organize Company Event" Subtasks:

- Book venue
- Send invitations
- Order catering
- Arrange transportation

Each subtask can have:

- Its own assignee
- Its own due date
- Attachments
- Comments

How to Add Subtasks

1. **Open the Task** you want to add subtasks to.
2. Look for the **Subtasks section** (icon with three dots connected by lines).
3. Click **Add Subtask** or press the shortcut **Tab + S**.
4. Type the subtask name and press **Enter**.
5. (Optional) Assign the subtask to a team member and set a due date.

Pro Tip: You can convert a subtask into a full task later if it becomes bigger than expected.

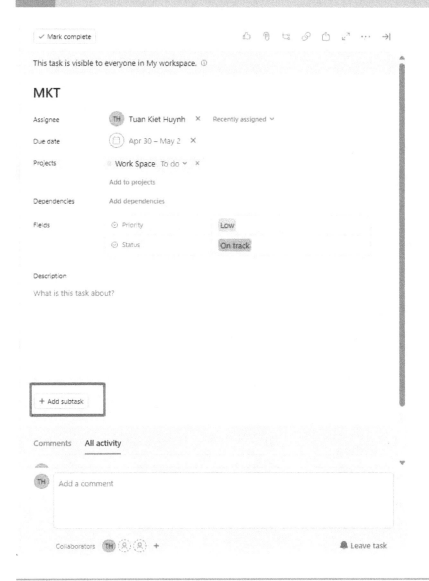

Organizing and Managing Subtasks

Adding More Details to Subtasks

Subtasks are not just simple checklists; they can be detailed action items.

For each subtask, you can:

- Add a full description

- Attach files

- Set priority labels

- Use custom fields

Using Sections for Subtasks

If you have too many subtasks, you can organize them into sections (in List view) for better clarity.

Example:

- Section: "Before Event"

  o Book venue

  o Hire photographer

- Section: "During Event"

  o Check audio/visual equipment

  o Manage registration table

- Section: "After Event"

  o Send thank-you emails

  o Collect feedback

Tracking Progress of Subtasks

When a parent task has subtasks:

- The task completion bar shows the progress as you complete subtasks.

- This visual indicator helps you quickly assess whether the overall task is on track.

Common Mistakes to Avoid with Tasks and Subtasks

- **Over-nesting subtasks.** Asana supports multiple levels of subtasks, but avoid going deeper than necessary (e.g., subtasks of subtasks of subtasks).

- **Not assigning subtasks.** Just like tasks, if a subtask is not assigned, it's easy to forget.

- **Using subtasks instead of tasks when collaboration is needed.** Remember, subtasks are hidden in project views by default unless explicitly added to projects.

Real-World Example: Adding Tasks and Subtasks

Scenario: Launching a New Website

Main Task: "Prepare Website Launch"

Subtasks:

- Write homepage content (Assignee: Content Team)

- Design landing pages (Assignee: Design Team)

- Set up hosting and domain (Assignee: IT Team)

- QA Testing (Assignee: QA Team)

- Final approval and go-live (Assignee: Project Manager)

Each subtask has a clear deliverable, owner, and deadline, ensuring that no critical steps are missed before the public launch.

Tips for Effective Task and Subtask Management

- Review your tasks and subtasks daily.

- Use "My Tasks" to manage personal assignments effectively.

- Leverage Asana notifications to stay updated on task changes.

- Keep task titles short but clear; use descriptions for more details.

- Regularly check if a subtask has grown enough to become a standalone task.

- Close completed tasks promptly to maintain a clean workspace.

Summary

Adding tasks and subtasks is the heart of using Asana effectively. When you carefully create clear tasks, assign ownership, set deadlines, and organize subtasks, you lay a strong foundation for managing projects and workflows successfully.

In the next section, we will dive into organizing your projects even more effectively by mastering **Sections**, **Columns**, and **different project views** in Asana.

2.1.2 Setting Assignees and Due Dates

In Asana, simply creating tasks is only the first step toward effective project management. To truly unlock the platform's potential, you must properly assign tasks to the right people and set clear due dates. These two actions transform a task from a passive note into a clear, actionable item, empowering your team to work efficiently and meet deadlines confidently.

In this section, we will dive deep into **how to assign tasks**, **how to set and manage due dates**, and **best practices for using these features** to streamline your workflows and improve project outcomes.

Why Setting Assignees and Due Dates Matters

Imagine you create a list of tasks for a big project. If no one knows who is responsible for what or when tasks are expected to be completed, confusion reigns. Work may fall through the cracks, deadlines get missed, and accountability disappears. Setting an **assignee** (the person responsible for completing the task) and a **due date** (the deadline by which the task must be finished) provides clarity and accountability for everyone involved.

Benefits of assigning tasks and setting due dates include:

- Clear responsibility and ownership
- Reduced misunderstandings
- Easier prioritization of work
- Better time management and resource allocation
- Improved collaboration and communication across teams

Now, let's learn exactly how to do it in Asana.

How to Assign Tasks in Asana

Assigning a task to someone is simple in Asana, but doing it thoughtfully is crucial.

Step-by-Step: Assigning a Task

1. **Create or Open a Task**: Either create a new task by clicking the **"+ Add Task"** button or open an existing task that you want to assign.

2. **Locate the Assignee Field**: In the task details pane (usually on the right side of the screen), you will see a field labeled **"Assignee"** at the top.

3. **Choose an Assignee**:

   o   Click on the Assignee field.

   o   Start typing the team member's name or email address.

   o   Select the correct person from the dropdown list that appears.

4. **Save Automatically**: Once selected, Asana automatically saves the assignee information. The assigned person will be notified through Asana (and possibly via email, depending on their settings).

Note:

- Each task in Asana can have **only one assignee**. This is intentional to ensure clear ownership.

- If multiple people need to work on a task, consider creating **subtasks** and assigning them individually.

Assigning Tasks Quickly

When working from the **List View** or **Board View**, you can also assign tasks more quickly without opening the task details:

- In List View, hover over the task, click the assignee icon, and select the person.

- In Board View, click directly on the task card, find the assignee icon, and choose the person.

How to Set Due Dates in Asana

Setting a due date provides a timeline for task completion, creating urgency and focus.

Step-by-Step: Setting a Due Date

1. **Create or Open a Task**: Just like with assigning a task, either create a new task or open an existing one.

2. **Locate the Due Date Field**: In the task details pane, find the field labeled **"Due Date"** right next to the Assignee field.

3. **Pick a Date**:

   o   Click on the Due Date field.

   o   A calendar will pop up.

   o   Select the date when the task should be completed.

4. **Optional: Set a Due Time**: If your team works with specific times, you can add a due time (e.g., complete by 5:00 PM).

5. **Save Automatically**: As soon as you select the date, Asana saves it automatically.

Setting a Due Date Range (Start Date and Due Date)

Some tasks take several days to complete. For these cases:

- Click **"Add Start Date"** (you'll find this option near the Due Date field).

- Set both a **Start Date** and a **Due Date** to define the work period.

This feature is particularly useful for complex tasks or tracking tasks across longer project timelines.

Advanced Options for Assigning and Scheduling

Recurring Tasks

In Asana, you can set tasks to repeat at regular intervals:

- Daily

- Weekly

- Monthly

- Custom schedules

How to Set Recurring Tasks:

- After setting a due date, click on the small arrow next to the date.

- Choose **"Set to Repeat"** and select the desired interval.

This is useful for repetitive tasks like weekly team meetings, monthly reports, or quarterly reviews.

Assigning Subtasks

If a task involves multiple steps or needs contributions from several team members:

- Create **subtasks** within the main task.

- Assign each subtask individually, complete with its own assignee and due date.

This keeps the work structured and ensures that everyone knows their specific role in completing the larger task.

Best Practices for Assigning Tasks and Setting Deadlines

Over time, mastering some strategic practices will help you and your team work more smoothly:

Be Specific About Ownership

Always ensure that tasks are assigned to the person **responsible for completing it**, not just overseeing it.

Set Realistic Deadlines

Avoid setting overly ambitious deadlines that could lead to unnecessary pressure and burnout. Allow for some buffer time whenever possible.

Prioritize Tasks Clearly

Use **Tags**, **Custom Fields**, or **Sections** to indicate priority levels. Example: Mark tasks as "High Priority", "Medium Priority", or "Low Priority."

Communicate Context and Expectations

Use the task description to explain:

- Why the task matters

- What is expected in the deliverable

- Any resources or attachments available

- Any dependencies (other tasks that must be completed first)

Update Due Dates When Needed

If a project timeline shifts, be proactive about updating due dates so the entire team stays aligned.

Avoid Over-Assigning

Be careful not to overload team members with too many tasks at once. Use Asana's **Workload View** (in Premium and higher plans) to monitor team capacity.

Common Mistakes to Avoid

1. **Leaving Tasks Unassigned**: A task without an owner tends to be forgotten.

2. **Setting Vague or No Due Dates**: Without a clear timeline, tasks may get endlessly postponed.

3. **Assigning Tasks to Multiple People**: Asana is designed for **single ownership**. Avoid "shared" ownership unless you structure it with subtasks.

4. **Neglecting to Communicate Changes**: If you change assignees or due dates, notify those involved — don't assume they'll notice the change on their own.

5. **Overcomplicating Simple Tasks**: Not every task needs a full description, multiple subtasks, or custom fields. Match the complexity to the task's real needs.

Examples: Assigning and Setting Deadlines in Real Scenarios

Here are a few real-world examples to show how this works:

Example 1: Content Creation

- **Task**: Write a blog post about Asana integrations.

- **Assignee**: Sarah (Content Writer)

- **Due Date**: June 15

- **Subtasks**:

  - Research integrations (Due June 10, assigned to John)

  - Draft blog post (Due June 12, assigned to Sarah)

  - Review and edit (Due June 14, assigned to Lisa)

Example 2: Event Planning

- **Task**: Organize Q3 Team Offsite

- **Assignee**: Kevin (Project Manager)

- **Due Date**: September 1

- **Subtasks**:

  - Book venue (Due July 1, assigned to Rachel)

  - Send invites (Due July 15, assigned to Mark)

  - Finalize agenda (Due August 15, assigned to Kevin)

Each person knows exactly what they are responsible for and by when.

Final Thoughts: The Foundation of Accountability

Assigning tasks and setting due dates may seem simple, but they form the backbone of effective work management in Asana. Without them, projects lack structure, and teams lose momentum.

By mastering these features early on, you build a culture of clarity, trust, and accountability — all essential ingredients for successful project execution.

In the next section, we'll explore how to organize projects even further by structuring them smartly with **Sections**, **Columns**, and flexible **Project Views**.

2.1.3 Using Task Descriptions and Attachments

Managing tasks efficiently is at the heart of any successful workflow, and Asana provides users with powerful tools to ensure tasks are clear, comprehensive, and actionable. Among these tools, **task descriptions** and **attachments** play a crucial role. They add depth, clarity, and necessary resources to tasks, turning simple to-do items into fully contextualized action points that anyone on the team can understand and act upon without needing additional meetings or explanations.

In this section, we will walk step-by-step through everything you need to know about **using task descriptions and attachments effectively** to enhance your Asana projects.

The Importance of Task Descriptions

A task without a description is like a map without landmarks. It might point you in the general direction, but it leaves too much room for confusion, misinterpretation, and mistakes. A well-written task description:

- Clarifies the objective of the task
- Provides step-by-step instructions
- Outlines expectations and deadlines
- Links to necessary references and resources
- Reduces the need for follow-up clarification

By investing a few minutes into writing clear descriptions, teams save hours of unnecessary communication and revisions later on.

How to Add a Task Description in Asana

When you create a new task in Asana, a description field is readily available. Here's how you can effectively use it:

1. **Create or Select a Task**
   - Navigate to your project and click on "Add Task."

    o   Alternatively, select an existing task you want to edit.

2. **Locate the Description Field**

    o   Upon opening the task pane on the right-hand side, you will see a large text box labeled "Description" under the task title.

3. **Enter Your Description**

    o   Write a clear, concise, and comprehensive explanation.

    o   Use bullet points or numbered lists if the task involves multiple steps.

    o   Highlight important deadlines or dependencies.

    o   Mention any team members involved or impacted.

4. **Formatting Tips**: Asana allows basic rich text formatting:

    o   **Bold**, *Italicize*, underline

    o   Create checklists

    o   Insert hyperlinks

    o   Add bullet points and numbered lists

    o   Use headings for better structure

To format text, use the toolbar that appears when you highlight your text inside the description field.

Best Practices for Writing Effective Task Descriptions

To maximize clarity and utility, consider these best practices:

- **Be Specific and Action-Oriented**: Avoid vague language. Instead of writing "Prepare the presentation," specify "Create a 10-slide presentation summarizing Q2 marketing campaign results."

- **Focus on Outcomes**: Clearly state what constitutes task completion.

- **Break Complex Tasks into Steps**: If a task has multiple components, list them clearly or even create subtasks.

- **Provide Context**: Explain why the task matters. Context motivates better work.

- **Reference Resources**: Mention any relevant documents, links, or tools needed to complete the task.

- **Use Consistent Language Across Teams**: Establish standardized task writing guidelines if possible, so everyone understands task instructions the same way.

Understanding and Using Attachments in Asana

While descriptions provide the "what" and "how," **attachments** provide the **supporting materials**. Attachments could be:

- Images

- PDFs

- Spreadsheets

- Word documents

- Design files

- Video clips

- Links to cloud resources

Adding attachments to a task ensures that anyone assigned the task has immediate access to the resources they need, without sifting through emails or separate cloud folders.

How to Attach Files to a Task

Adding attachments in Asana is straightforward:

1. **Open a Task**: Navigate to the task you want to work on.

2. **Click the Attachment Icon**: The paperclip icon ("Attach file") appears near the top of the task pane.

3. **Choose Your Source**: You can upload from:

   o   Your computer

- Google Drive
- Dropbox
- Box
- OneDrive
- Direct link (for online resources)

4. **Upload and Attach**: Select your file, and it will immediately attach to the task. You can attach multiple files to a single task.

Managing and Using Attachments Efficiently

Once attachments are uploaded:

- They appear below the task description.
- Team members can preview files without downloading.
- You can add comments directly referencing attached files.
- Asana will generate thumbnails for image files for easier identification.

Important Tips:

- **Version Control:** Upload the most current version of a document. Label files with version numbers if multiple iterations are expected.
- **Organize Files:** If a task involves several files, use clear naming conventions (e.g., "Marketing_Plan_V1" vs "Final_Marketing_Plan").
- **Update Regularly:** If a document becomes outdated, upload the updated version and note the change in the task comments.

Using Descriptions and Attachments Together

The best use of Asana's task management features comes when you **combine rich descriptions with appropriate attachments**. Here's an example:

Task Title: "Draft Q2 Marketing Campaign Overview"
Description:

- Review Q1 metrics (attached report)

- Develop a campaign outline (5 sections: Objectives, Audience, Channels, Budget, Timeline)

- Refer to the style guide (attached document)

- Due by Friday 5 PM for initial review

Attachments:

- "Q1_Marketing_Results.pdf"

- "Marketing_Style_Guide.docx"

This combination gives the assignee everything needed to get started immediately, dramatically increasing productivity.

Real-World Examples: Task Descriptions and Attachments

Example 1: Product Launch Task

- **Description:**
  Finalize product page content. Review attached draft, update copy to include new features outlined in the marketing brief.

- **Attachments:**

    o   Product_Page_Draft.docx

    o   Marketing_Brief_Q2.pdf

Example 2: Event Planning Task

- **Description:**
  Confirm venue booking for the company retreat. Ensure dates match event schedule. Update retreat checklist accordingly.

- **Attachments:**

    o   Venue_Options.xlsx

    o   Event_Schedule.docx

Common Mistakes to Avoid

- **Overloading the Description Field**: Keep it focused. If you need to provide lots of supporting materials, use attachments instead.

- **Attaching Unnecessary Files**: Attach only files relevant to the task. Irrelevant attachments cause confusion.

- **Failing to Update Attachments**: Old versions of files can derail an entire project. Always ensure uploads are up-to-date.

- **Writing Vague Descriptions**: "Review this" or "Check document" without specifying what to look for wastes time and frustrates team members.

Summary and Key Takeaways

- Task descriptions provide the **what, why, and how** of a task.

- Attachments provide the **resources** needed to complete the task.

- A clear description combined with organized attachments results in **higher task completion rates, fewer miscommunications**, and **better project outcomes**.

- Regularly updating both descriptions and attachments is crucial for maintaining project momentum.

Actionable Checklist: Creating Effective Tasks in Asana

- Write clear, outcome-focused descriptions.
- Break tasks into steps if necessary.
- Attach only the essential files.
- Use formatting to make descriptions easier to scan.
- Reference important deadlines and dependencies.
- Keep attachments up-to-date.
- Maintain a consistent description style across the team.

2.2 Organizing Projects Effectively

2.2.1 Using Sections and Columns

When managing complex projects in Asana, **organization is everything**. Without a clear structure, even the most ambitious projects can quickly become overwhelming and chaotic. Fortunately, Asana provides powerful tools — **Sections** and **Columns** — that help you organize your work visually and logically. In this section, we'll dive deep into how to use these features to build projects that are clear, actionable, and adaptable to your team's needs.

Understanding Sections and Columns in Asana

Before we get hands-on, it's important to understand what **Sections** and **Columns** actually are within Asana:

- **Sections**:
  In Asana's **List View**, Sections are used to divide a project into different groups of tasks. Think of them as headers or categories that allow you to cluster related tasks together.

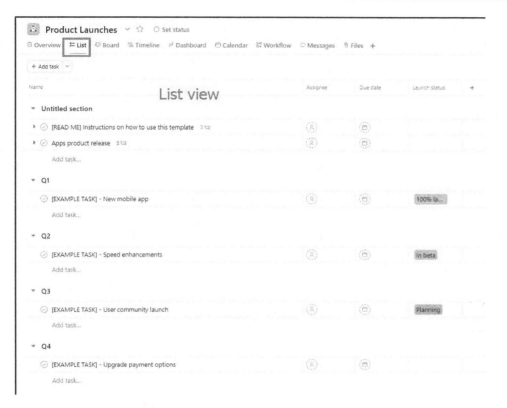

- **Columns**:

  In Asana's **Board View**, Columns serve a similar function. They act as lanes or stages in a workflow — a visual kanban-style arrangement where tasks move from one column to another as they progress.

Although they are called differently depending on the view, **Sections and Columns share the same purpose**: **to create a meaningful structure** for your project, so tasks aren't just floating around in one endless list.

Why Organization Matters

Organizing projects with Sections and Columns is not just about aesthetics. It directly impacts your team's performance:

- **Improved clarity**: Everyone knows where a task belongs and what phase it's in.

- **Easier prioritization**: You can quickly scan which tasks are urgent, pending, or completed.

- **Streamlined workflows**: Logical steps are easier to follow, especially for complex projects.

- **Enhanced collaboration**: Team members can understand the overall project structure at a glance, reducing communication gaps.

- **Better reporting**: Well-organized projects make it easier to extract insights through reports and dashboards.

Poorly organized projects, on the other hand, often result in missed deadlines, duplicated work, or confusion about priorities.

How to Create Sections in List View

Creating Sections in List View is simple but powerful:

1. **Open Your Project in List View**: Make sure you are viewing your project in "List" format. You can switch views using the toolbar at the top.

2. **Add a Section**:

   o Click the "Add Section" button located above the list of tasks.

   o Alternatively, you can use the shortcut Tab + N to quickly create a new Section.

o Name your Section clearly and descriptively — for example: "To Do," "In Progress," or "Completed."

3. **Organize Tasks Under Sections**:

   o Drag and drop tasks under the appropriate Section.

   o You can move Sections around by clicking and dragging their headers.

4. **Customize Your Sections**:

   o Use emoji or special formatting (like CAPITAL LETTERS) to make Section headers stand out.

   o Align Sections with phases of your project, categories of work, team members, or priorities.

Pro Tip: You can collapse Sections when you don't need to see all tasks, keeping your project view tidy.

How to Create Columns in Board View

If you're more visually oriented, Board View offers a kanban-like experience:

1. **Switch to Board View**: Click on "Board" at the top of your project screen.

2. **Create New Columns**:

   o Click "Add Column" on the right side of your Board.

   o Name your Columns according to your workflow stages (e.g., "Backlog," "Ready to Start," "In Review," "Completed").

3. **Moving Tasks Across Columns**:

   o Drag tasks from one Column to another as their status changes.

   o This is particularly powerful for teams using Agile or Scrum methodologies.

4. **Customize Column Settings**:

   o Use color-coded tags within tasks to add even more clarity.

      o   Set up Rules (automation) so that, for example, when a task moves into "Done," it automatically marks itself as complete.

👉 **Pro Tip**: You can also convert a Board View back into List View if you later decide a different visual organization better suits your team.

Best Practices for Structuring Your Project with Sections and Columns

Let's talk about how you can **strategically structure your project** for maximum efficiency:

1. Mirror Your Workflow

Your Sections/Columns should **mirror the natural stages** of your workflow. If you are managing a content calendar, for example, your Sections might be:

- Idea
- Writing
- Editing
- Scheduled
- Published

If you're managing an IT helpdesk, your Columns could be:

- New Ticket
- Assigned
- In Progress
- Awaiting Feedback
- Resolved

Align your project structure with real-world processes, not just arbitrary categories.

---

2. Keep It Simple

Avoid overcomplicating your Sections or Columns. Too many subdivisions can become confusing and defeat the purpose of organization.

☑ A good rule of thumb: **3–7 Sections/Columns** are ideal for most projects. 🚫 Avoid having so many that team members have to scroll endlessly to find where their task fits.

---

3. Use Naming Conventions

Create consistent, easy-to-understand Section and Column names. Some examples:

- Always use verbs ("To Do," "In Progress," "Completed").

- If you use statuses, stick with the same terminology across multiple projects.

- If managing priorities, be clear: "High Priority," "Medium Priority," "Low Priority."

---

4. Incorporate Visual Aids

Adding emojis, prefixes, or specific formatting can help users quickly recognize Sections and Columns. For example:

- 🚀 Launch Phase

- 📝 Content Drafting

- ☑ QA Approved

This enhances usability, especially for large projects.

---

5. Standardize Across Teams

If your organization has multiple teams, consider creating **standard templates** for how Sections and Columns should be set up. This reduces onboarding time for new team members and creates consistency.

Example template for a software development team:

- Icebox

- Ready for Development
- In Development
- Code Review
- Deployed
- Archived

Common Mistakes to Avoid

Even experienced users sometimes misuse Sections and Columns. Watch out for:

- **Too many tasks under one Section/Column**: Break large groups into smaller, manageable sets.
- **Sections without tasks**: Empty Sections clutter the workspace and confuse team members.
- **Non-actionable names**: If a Section title isn't clear, it can slow decision-making.
- **Changing structure mid-project without communication**: Always alert your team if you restructure a project so they can adapt.

Real-World Examples: Organizing Projects

Let's look at two real-world examples of how Sections and Columns can structure a project effectively.

Example 1: Marketing Campaign Launch

Sections/Columns:

- Brainstorm Ideas
- Campaign Planning
- Content Creation
- Launch Preparation
- Live Campaign

- Post-Campaign Analysis

Tasks would move systematically from ideation to analysis, keeping the team focused on the right stage at the right time.

Example 2: Product Development

Sections/Columns:

- Feature Backlog
- Design in Progress
- Development in Progress
- Testing
- Released

This creates a **clear Agile workflow** that multiple teams (designers, developers, testers) can work within simultaneously.

Tips for Managing Sections and Columns Over Time

- **Review periodically**: As your project evolves, check if your Sections/Columns still fit the process.

- **Archive old Sections**: If certain phases are no longer relevant, archive or delete them to declutter.

- **Celebrate milestones**: Move completed tasks to a "Celebrated!" Column or Section — it can boost team morale!

Conclusion

Organizing your project effectively with **Sections and Columns** is a game-changer in Asana.
Done well, it turns a basic list of tasks into a living, breathing roadmap for your team's success.

Whether you're managing a personal project or leading a large team initiative, learning to **structure your projects thoughtfully** will improve visibility, accountability, and overall project   outcomes.
Master this skill now, and you'll find yourself — and your team — working smarter, faster, and with far less stress.

Next Section: In the next part (**2.2.2 Prioritizing and Tagging Tasks**), we'll explore how to set priorities and categorize tasks to take your project management to the next level.

2.2.2 Prioritizing and Tagging Tasks

In any project management system, knowing **what to do first** and **how to group similar tasks** are two fundamental pillars of efficiency. In Asana, this is achieved through **Prioritizing** and **Tagging**. Mastering these simple but powerful features will transform the way you handle projects — helping you and your team stay focused, aligned, and agile. Let's dive deep into how you can prioritize tasks and use tags effectively in Asana to streamline your project organization.

Understanding the Need for Prioritization and Tagging

Before learning how to use the tools, it's important to understand **why** prioritization and tagging matter:

- **Prioritization** ensures that critical work is completed on time and that your team's attention is focused where it is most needed.

- **Tagging** enables easy sorting, filtering, and identifying of tasks across projects, ensuring related items are grouped even if they reside in different projects.

Together, these practices help prevent overwhelm, reduce missed deadlines, and create a clear roadmap for execution.

Prioritizing Tasks in Asana

Prioritization helps answer a simple but critical question: **"What should I work on next?"**

While Asana does not have a default "Priority" field visible on every task, it provides **several flexible ways** to prioritize work depending on the complexity of your project or team's needs.

Methods for Prioritizing Tasks

1. Using Sections and Custom Fields

One of the most straightforward ways to prioritize tasks is to create **Sections** like:

- High Priority
- Medium Priority
- Low Priority

You can easily drag and drop tasks between sections as their priority changes.

Another method is to create a **Custom Field** named "Priority" with dropdown options (High, Medium, Low). This allows you to sort and filter tasks by their priority across different views (List, Board, Calendar, etc.).

Steps to Add a Priority Custom Field:

1. Open your Project.
2. Click on **Customize** in the upper right corner.
3. Under **Fields**, click **Add Field → Create New Field**.
4. Name it "Priority" and choose **Dropdown** type.
5. Add values like "High", "Medium", and "Low" (you can even assign colors).
6. Save and apply to your project.

Pro Tip: When using Custom Fields, you can later **filter** your project view to only show high-priority tasks, making daily stand-ups or weekly planning much more efficient.

2. Visual Priority with Task Colors

Although Asana doesn't allow coloring tasks natively based on importance, you can simulate this by combining Custom Fields with colored labels or by using **Tag Colors** (we'll explore this in the tagging section).

When properly used, **visual cues** speed up your ability to scan and detect what needs immediate action.

3. Due Dates as Implicit Priority

Another implicit method of setting priorities is via **Due Dates**. Tasks with imminent deadlines can be considered a de facto higher priority. In the **Calendar View** or **My Tasks** sorted by due date, Asana naturally surfaces upcoming deadlines to the top.

However, due dates alone can be misleading if urgent tasks don't have early deadlines. This is why combining due dates **with priority fields** is often the best approach.

Tagging Tasks in Asana

Tagging is Asana's way of giving tasks an **additional label** that can:

- Group them across different projects.

- Mark them with special attributes.

- Make them easily searchable.

Tags are flexible — they don't affect the project hierarchy — but they add powerful metadata to tasks.

Creating and Using Tags

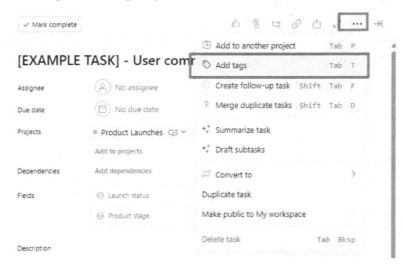

To add a tag to a task:

1. Open a task.

2. Click the three dots (•••) in the task toolbar.

3. Choose **Add Tag**.

4. Create a new tag or search for an existing one.

Once tags are applied, you can click on any tag to see a list of **all tasks** across your entire Asana account that share that tag.

Best Practices for Tagging

1. Create a Clear Tagging Convention

Without a system, tags can quickly become chaotic. To prevent confusion:

- Agree on naming standards (e.g., singular vs plural forms, capitalization).

- Avoid creating duplicate tags with similar names like "Urgent" vs "urgent".

Example of clear conventions:

- Priority Levels: #urgent, #important, #lowpriority

- Task Types: #bug, #feature, #research

- Status Labels: #waiting, #inreview, #completedexternal

Tip: Prefixing tags with a symbol like "#" or categorizing by theme can help organize them better.

2. Use Tags to Track Special Categories Across Projects

Tags are perfect for:

- Marking **Bugs** across multiple product projects.

- Highlighting **Tasks requiring legal review** in different marketing campaigns.

- Tagging **Client Requests** across unrelated service projects.

Because tasks live inside specific projects, tags provide a cross-sectional way to retrieve information that would otherwise be siloed.

3. Color Coding Tags for Better Visual Management

Asana allows you to **assign colors** to tags, which show up as small bubbles next to the task title. Use color coding smartly:

- **Red** for urgent issues.

- **Blue** for informational tasks.

- **Green** for completed, signed-off items.

This visual layering helps you quickly spot patterns and areas of attention in your workflow.

Combining Prioritization and Tagging for Maximum Impact

The real magic happens when you **use prioritization and tagging together**.

For example:

- A task can belong to a **high-priority section** AND have the tag **#urgent**.

- A bug fix in a development project can have a **Priority: High** custom field AND be tagged as **#bug**.

- You could even set up a **Rule** (using Asana's automation) that whenever a task is tagged #urgent, it moves automatically to the **High Priority** section.

This layered system ensures no important task slips through the cracks.

Advanced Tips for Power Users

Use Rules for Automatic Prioritization

If you're on a paid Asana plan, you can create **Rules** such as:

- When a task is added with the tag #urgent, set its Priority field to High.

- When a task due date is within 2 days, automatically move it to the "Urgent" Section.

These automations reduce manual work and create consistency across your project.

Build Custom Reporting Based on Priority and Tags

With Asana's **Advanced Search** and **Reporting Features**, you can build custom dashboards showing:

- All high-priority tasks across all projects.

- All tasks tagged as #inreview.

- All tasks assigned to a specific teammate that are tagged #urgent.

Dynamic reporting ensures you always have a pulse on the most critical areas of your organization.

Common Mistakes to Avoid

- **Overusing Tags:** Too many tags can create noise rather than clarity. Stick to a purposeful tagging system.

- **Neglecting Prioritization Updates:** A task's priority can change over time. Make updating priorities part of your weekly review.

- **Inconsistent Tagging Across Teams:** Without a unified standard, tags lose their value. Always align with your team's tagging strategy.

- **Forgetting to Review Tagged Tasks:** It's easy to tag tasks and forget them. Set reminders to review high-importance tags periodically.

Conclusion: Making Prioritization and Tagging Work for You

Prioritization and tagging in Asana are deceptively simple features that, when used correctly, unlock a whole new level of control over your work. By systematically organizing tasks with clear priorities and smart tags, you:

- Reduce chaos and confusion.

- Empower faster decision-making.

- Enable smarter cross-project navigation.

- Ensure nothing critical gets overlooked.

Like any tool, the power of Asana comes not just from its features, but from **how well you and your team use them consistently**.

With the techniques covered in this section, you're now equipped to bring clarity, efficiency, and focus to your Asana projects — one prioritized, well-tagged task at a time.

2.2.3 Project Views: List, Board, Calendar, Timeline

When it comes to managing projects, **visibility** is everything. In Asana, you are not limited to a one-size-fits-all approach; instead, Asana offers four powerful project views—**List, Board, Calendar, and Timeline**—to accommodate different working styles and project types. Understanding how and when to use each view will greatly enhance your ability to organize, track, and deliver projects successfully.

In this section, we'll take a deep dive into each project view, examining their strengths, use cases, and best practices.

Understanding Project Views in Asana

Project views in Asana are simply different ways of visualizing the same underlying data— your tasks and project structures. Switching between views doesn't change the content of your tasks; it changes how you **interact** with and **perceive** your project.

Different types of teams, tasks, and projects will naturally align better with different views. Whether you are organizing a product launch, managing an editorial calendar, or planning a marketing campaign, choosing the right view can streamline your workflow.

Let's explore each view one by one.

List View: Structured and Detail-Oriented

The **List View** is the default view for most Asana users, especially those who prefer a structured, spreadsheet-like format. Think of it like a dynamic, interactive checklist.

Key Features of List View

- **Hierarchical Structure:** Organize tasks into sections (or columns) and subtasks.

- **Customizable Columns:** Add fields like Priority, Status, Due Date, Assignee, Tags, and Custom Fields.

- **Sorting and Filtering:** Quickly sort tasks by due date, priority, or assignee.

- **Bulk Actions:** Select multiple tasks to update assignees, deadlines, or status simultaneously.

When to Use List View

- Projects that require **sequential steps** (e.g., onboarding new employees).

- Tasks with detailed attributes (multiple assignees, dependencies, tags).

- Teams that value a **clear, comprehensive** overview of work.

Best Practices for List View

- Use **Sections** to logically group tasks (e.g., "To Do", "In Progress", "Completed").

- Always assign due dates and assignees to avoid orphaned tasks.

- Regularly update task statuses to reflect progress.

Board View: Visual and Agile-Friendly

Inspired by **Kanban methodology**, the **Board View** presents your tasks as cards organized into columns. It's an excellent choice for teams that like to **visualize workflow stages**.

Key Features of Board View

- **Drag-and-Drop:** Move tasks across columns effortlessly.

- **Custom Columns:** Define stages like "Backlog", "In Progress", "Review", "Done."

- **WIP Limits:** (Work-in-Progress) Visual limitation of tasks per stage.

- **Card Details:** Click on a task card to view or edit all task information.

When to Use Board View

- Projects requiring **workflow visualization** (e.g., product development, bug tracking).

- Agile and Scrum teams managing sprints.

- Editorial calendars (e.g., blog posts moving from draft to published).

Best Practices for Board View

- Clearly label columns based on project phases.

- Limit the number of tasks in "In Progress" to prevent bottlenecks.

- Use color coding (via Custom Fields) to differentiate types of tasks.

Calendar View: Time-Based Planning

The **Calendar View** displays all project tasks across a monthly or weekly calendar grid, based on their due dates. It's perfect for planning deadlines, campaigns, and deliverables.

Key Features of Calendar View

- **Drag-and-Drop Rescheduling:** Easily adjust deadlines by dragging tasks.

- **Event Visualization:** See workload distribution over time.

- **Integration Friendly:** Sync with Google Calendar, Outlook, and more.

- **Filters:** Focus on specific assignees or task types.

When to Use Calendar View

- Planning time-sensitive projects (e.g., event planning, marketing campaigns).

- Managing deadlines and deliverables for multiple team members.

- Visualizing project workload over a period.

Best Practices for Calendar View

- Regularly review your team's Calendar to ensure no overlaps or unrealistic deadlines.

- Color-code tasks using Custom Fields to identify priority or task type.

- Use recurring tasks for regular events (e.g., weekly reports, monthly meetings).

Timeline View: Gantt Chart Power for Complex Projects

The **Timeline View** provides a **Gantt chart**-like visualization of your project. It is ideal for planning **multi-phase projects** with dependencies between tasks.

Key Features of Timeline View

- **Task Dependencies:** Link tasks so one can't start until another finishes.
- **Zoom Levels:** View your project over days, weeks, or months.
- **Drag-and-Drop Rescheduling:** Adjust timelines with simple movements.
- **Critical Path Identification:** Recognize bottlenecks that could delay your project.

When to Use Timeline View

- Complex projects involving multiple teams (e.g., product launches, construction projects).
- Projects where **task dependencies** must be managed carefully.
- High-stakes projects with **tight deadlines**.

Best Practices for Timeline View

- Map out all critical milestones before adding dependent tasks.
- Set clear start and end dates for every task.
- Regularly review the Timeline to catch schedule risks early.

Comparing Project Views: Which One Should You Use?

Aspect	List View	Board View	Calendar View	Timeline View
Best For	Detailed task management	Workflow visualization	Deadline planning	Complex project scheduling
Suitable Projects	Checklists, admin work	Agile projects, marketing	Event planning, content calendars	Product launches, engineering
Team Style	Detail-oriented	Visual thinkers	Time-focused	Strategic planners
Key Strength	Clear overview	Easy task movement	Date visibility	Dependency management

You can switch views any time without losing data, and even combine them for maximum effectiveness.

For example, use **List View** to add detailed information, **Board View** to manage status, **Calendar View** to track deadlines, and **Timeline View** to plan phases.

Tips for Choosing and Using Project Views

- **Mix and Match:** Don't limit your team to just one view. Different members may prefer different perspectives.

- **Establish Norms:** Agree on which view will be the "default" for team updates or meetings.

- **Training:** Offer short internal training sessions on navigating each view.

- **Customization:** Use Custom Fields, Tags, and Rules to enhance the functionality of all views.

- **Review Regularly:** Reassess your choice of views as project needs evolve.

Conclusion: Project Views Empower You to Work Smarter

Choosing the right project view in Asana is like picking the right lens to see your work. Each view offers a unique perspective, and mastering them will empower you to **organize projects more effectively, collaborate better with your team, and achieve your goals with clarity and efficiency**.

Remember:

👉 List for structure,
👉 Board for workflow,
👉 Calendar for timing,
👉 Timeline for strategy.

Leverage these views according to your project's needs, and you'll be on your way to building **your perfect workflow** in Asana!

2.3 Tracking Progress

2.3.1 Status Updates and Progress Reports

Tracking progress is a crucial part of successful project management. Without clear visibility into where a project stands, it becomes difficult to identify potential roadblocks, celebrate milestones, and ensure that everyone is aligned towards shared goals. In Asana, you have a variety of powerful features specifically designed to track project progress effortlessly. This section will guide you through using **Status Updates** and **Progress Reports** effectively to keep your team informed, motivated, and on track.

Understanding the Importance of Progress Tracking

Before diving into the tools, it's important to understand why tracking progress is vital:

- **Transparency:** Everyone on the team knows exactly how the project is advancing.
- **Accountability:** Team members are more likely to complete their tasks on time when they know their work contributes to overall project health.
- **Risk Management:** Early detection of delays or problems allows for quick action.
- **Motivation:** Visualizing progress can boost team morale and encourage momentum.

Asana makes it simple to turn these principles into daily practice.

Using Status Updates in Asana

What Are Status Updates?

Status Updates are project-level communications that summarize the current state of a project, highlight key achievements, flag risks, and outline next steps. They provide a structured, consistent way to keep stakeholders informed without needing constant meetings or emails.

Creating a Status Update

1. **Navigate to the Project:** Open the project you want to update.

2. **Click on "Progress" Tab:** On the top menu inside your project, you'll find a "Progress" tab. Click it to view the project's overall status.

3. **Click "Update Status":** This opens a status update form where you can choose a status (On Track, At Risk, Off Track, or Complete) and add a written update.

4. **Write Your Update:** Your update should typically include:

   o **Summary:** One or two sentences explaining the current situation.

   o **Highlights:** Key accomplishments since the last update.

   o **Challenges:** Problems or risks the team should be aware of.

   o **Next Steps:** Immediate upcoming priorities.

5. **Add Visuals (Optional):** You can attach charts, images, or graphs to make your updates more engaging and easier to digest.

6. **Share the Update:** After writing the update, you can post it for the project team, and it will be archived for historical reference.

Best Practices for Writing Status Updates

- **Keep It Brief but Informative:** People should be able to understand the project status in under two minutes.

- **Be Honest and Clear:** If there are risks or delays, state them openly.

- **Highlight Both Successes and Challenges:** Balance celebrating progress with addressing problems.

- **Maintain a Regular Rhythm:** Weekly or bi-weekly updates keep momentum and visibility high.

Interpreting Project Status Colors

When you set the status, Asana uses color coding:

- **Green ("On Track")** – Everything is going according to plan.

- **Yellow ("At Risk")** – Some issues could impact the project but are manageable.

- **Red ("Off Track")** – Major problems threatening the success of the project.

- **Blue ("Complete")** – The project is finished.

These colors give a quick visual cue to anyone viewing the project, even without reading the full update.

Tracking Progress with Progress Reports

While status updates are manual and narrative-driven, Asana also provides **automated tools** to track ongoing project health in more quantifiable ways through Progress Reports.

Understanding Progress Reports

Progress Reports in Asana give a **snapshot view** of:

- Completed tasks

- Remaining tasks

- Milestones achieved

- Tasks overdue

- Overall project trends over time

These reports provide hard data to back up the narrative given in a status update.

How to Access Progress Reports

1. **Go to the Project Dashboard:** Select your project and open the "Dashboard" tab.

2. **View Auto-Generated Charts:** Here you'll find visual reports like:

   o Task completion charts

   o Burn-up and burn-down charts

   o Milestone achievements

   o Overdue task lists

   o Tasks created vs. tasks completed graphs

3. **Customize Your View:** You can add custom charts or rearrange widgets depending on the metrics you want to monitor closely.

Customizing Progress Reports

Asana allows you to **build custom dashboards** using:

- **Pie Charts:** Great for seeing task distribution by status or assignee.
- **Bar Graphs:** Perfect for tracking overdue tasks across team members.
- **Line Charts:** Excellent for visualizing project trends over time.

Custom Fields can also be used to categorize tasks and build highly specific reports, such as tracking task completion by department, priority, or client.

Combining Status Updates and Progress Reports for Maximum Impact

Using both **narrative updates** and **data-driven reports** together creates a comprehensive project tracking system:

- Use **Status Updates** to tell the story of the project: challenges, wins, team spirit.
- Use **Progress Reports** to provide the numbers behind that story.

When combined, they offer a powerful way to communicate project health to stakeholders at all levels—executives, managers, and team members alike.

Real-World Example: Weekly Project Check-ins Using Asana

Here's a simple weekly routine you can implement:

- **Monday Morning:** Check Progress Reports to understand where things stand.
- **Tuesday:** Follow up on overdue tasks with assigned team members.
- **Thursday Afternoon:** Write a quick draft of the Status Update based on key highlights and challenges seen in the reports.
- **Friday Morning:** Post the Status Update and schedule a 15-minute team meeting (optional) to review together.

This keeps everyone aligned without overwhelming the team with excessive meetings.

Common Mistakes When Tracking Progress (and How to Avoid Them)

1. **Infrequent Updates:**

   ○ Solution: Set a recurring reminder to post updates.

2. **Overly Optimistic Reporting:**

   ○ Solution: Be realistic, acknowledge risks openly.

3. **Ignoring Data Trends:**

   ○ Solution: Regularly check dashboards and reports, not just written updates.

4. **Lack of Accountability:**

   ○ Solution: Link task owners to specific deliverables clearly.

5. **Not Celebrating Milestones:**

   ○ Solution: Use Asana milestones and celebrate when teams hit key targets!

Pro Tips for Expert Progress Tracking

- **Use Milestones Strategically:** Mark key phases or deliveries, not just arbitrary moments.

- **Automate Reminders:** Asana's "Rules" feature can automatically remind assignees about overdue tasks.

- **Color-Code Projects:** Use project colors strategically to reflect urgency or phase.

- **Link Projects to Portfolios:** If you manage multiple projects, Portfolios provide a birds-eye view across everything.

- **Integrate Reporting Tools:** Tools like Tableau or Power BI can integrate with Asana for even deeper reporting if needed.

Conclusion: Mastering Progress Tracking in Asana

Progress tracking in Asana is not just about checking boxes—it's about creating clarity, accountability, and momentum. By mastering both Status Updates and Progress Reports, you empower your team to stay aligned, informed, and focused on outcomes. When used thoughtfully, Asana becomes more than a task manager—it becomes the heartbeat of your team's success.

Next, we'll explore how to build custom workflows tailored to your specific needs in Chapter 3.

2.3.2 Using Milestones

Milestones are key points within a project that mark significant achievements, deadlines, or turning points. In Asana, milestones provide visual markers that help teams and stakeholders stay aligned on major progress points and overall project health. Proper use of milestones transforms a regular task list into a powerful project roadmap, giving everyone involved a clear view of where they are and what's coming next.

In this section, we'll explore the importance of milestones, how to set them up in Asana, best practices for their use, and common mistakes to avoid. We'll also walk through real-world examples to illustrate their practical impact.

Understanding the Role of Milestones

Before diving into the how-to, it's important to understand **why milestones matter**:

- **Clarity**: Milestones clearly indicate what the major deliverables are.
- **Motivation**: Reaching a milestone can boost team morale.
- **Accountability**: Milestones encourage regular project reviews and adjustments.
- **Communication**: They serve as simple, visible markers for updates to stakeholders.
- **Risk Management**: Regular milestone tracking helps identify delays early.

In Asana, milestones aren't separate from tasks — they are a special type of task with a different visual indicator (usually represented with a diamond icon) that signals significance.

How to Create a Milestone in Asana

Setting up milestones is easy, but strategic placement is crucial. Here's a step-by-step guide:

Step 1: Open Your Project

Navigate to the project where you want to add a milestone. Ensure you are in a view that shows tasks, such as List View, Board View, or Timeline View.

Step 2: Create a New Task

Click the **"+ Add Task"** button. Name the task something clear and specific, reflecting the major event or deliverable it represents.

Example:
Instead of naming a milestone "Phase 1 Done," a better label would be "Complete User Research Phase."

Step 3: Convert the Task to a Milestone

After creating the task:

- Click into the task details.

- Find the option labeled **"Mark as Milestone."**

- Select it, and the task will visually change into a milestone (diamond icon).

Alternatively, in Timeline View, you can right-click on a task bar and select **"Mark as Milestone."**

Step 4: Assign and Set a Due Date

Milestones, like tasks, should have:

- A clear assignee (even if it's just for monitoring purposes).
- A specific due date to ensure time-sensitive tracking.

Without a due date, a milestone loses its ability to help with schedule visibility.

Best Practices for Using Milestones

Simply adding milestones isn't enough — **strategic use** is what turns milestones into a real asset.

1. Tie Milestones to Deliverables, Not Activities

Good milestones reflect *outcomes* rather than actions.

Example:

- ✗ Poor: "Hold Team Meeting" (activity)
- ✓ Better: "Finalize Project Scope After Team Meeting" (outcome)

2. Space Milestones Throughout the Project Timeline

Milestones should not be clumped together. Instead, spread them evenly across your project to maintain consistent tracking.

- Early Milestone: Requirements finalized
- Midpoint Milestone: Prototype completed

- Final Milestone: Product launch

3. Communicate Around Milestones

Make milestones part of regular updates:

- Reference upcoming and completed milestones in project meetings.
- Use them in Asana's **Status Updates** feature to show overall progress.
- Tag stakeholders or clients directly on milestone tasks when updates are needed.

4. Align Milestones with Stakeholder Reviews

Whenever possible, align milestones with critical review points like:

- Approval checkpoints
- Budget reviews
- Key client presentations

This way, milestone completion naturally triggers required reviews.

5. Color-Code or Prioritize Milestones

In busy projects, it can be easy to miss a milestone. You can:

- Apply a **specific color tag** to milestones.
- Add **priority indicators** (like emojis 🚀 ✅ 🔴) in milestone task titles.
- Create a **Milestones Section** at the top of the project to gather them.

Examples of Effective Milestone Use

Let's walk through a few different types of projects:

1. Software Development Project

- Kick-off Meeting Held 🎯
- Alpha Version Completed 🎯
- Beta Testing Begins 🎯

- Final Code Freeze ◎
- Product Launch ◎

Each of these represents a major deliverable or checkpoint.

2. Marketing Campaign

- Campaign Strategy Finalized
- Creative Assets Approved
- Ads Launched
- Mid-campaign Performance Review
- Campaign Wrap-up Report Delivered

Notice how each is tangible and reviewable.

3. Event Planning

- Venue Booked
- Speakers Confirmed
- Attendee Registration Open
- Final Rehearsal Completed
- Event Day Execution

Here, milestones help ensure the timeline remains tightly on track.

Tracking Milestones in Asana Views

Milestones can be viewed across various Asana layouts:

1. List View

Milestones appear alongside tasks but are easily spotted thanks to their diamond icons. You can also create a separate Section just for milestones.

2. Timeline View

In Timeline, milestones appear as **diamond shapes** on the project's timeline bar. This helps immediately visualize the sequence of major achievements relative to all project tasks.

Tip: In Timeline View, you can adjust milestone dates by dragging and dropping the diamond markers.

3. Calendar View

Milestones show up on their assigned due dates, offering a quick high-level check of key upcoming events.

Common Mistakes to Avoid When Using Milestones

While milestones are powerful, poor implementation can lead to confusion or inefficiency. Watch out for these pitfalls:

1. Using Too Many Milestones

If everything is a milestone, nothing feels significant. Reserve milestones for **truly critical points**.

2. Not Assigning Owners

Milestones without a responsible person often go unnoticed. Assign someone, even if their role is only to monitor the completion.

3. No Due Dates

Milestones without deadlines lose much of their usefulness in keeping projects on track.

4. Confusing Activities with Outcomes

Remember: a milestone should represent a **state achieved**, not just an action taken.

Advanced Tip: Linking Milestones with Dependencies

To add even more structure, you can set up **task dependencies**:

- Make certain tasks dependent on the completion of a milestone.

- This automatically prevents teams from moving forward on work that shouldn't begin before a key event.

Example:

The task "Launch Public Beta" should be **blocked** by the milestone "Beta Approval Finalized."

Dependencies can be set by:

- Opening a task

- Clicking **"Add Dependency"** and selecting the related milestone

This keeps project flow logical and controlled.

Final Thoughts on Milestones

Milestones are not just symbolic checkmarks. In Asana, they are active management tools that offer clarity, boost team alignment, and improve project delivery.

When used thoughtfully, milestones serve as **beacons** that guide your project from start to finish — helping teams celebrate wins, spot problems early, and stay motivated along the way.

As you continue building your projects in Asana, make milestones an essential part of your workflow design. You'll find that they bring structure, visibility, and momentum to even the most complex initiatives.

Coming Next: In the next section, we will explore **2.3.3 Project Dashboards**, where you will learn how to build real-time visual reporting for even deeper project insights!

2.3.3 Project Dashboards

In any project management system, the ability to **track progress visually** is essential for keeping everyone aligned and for ensuring that objectives are met on time. In Asana, **Project Dashboards** serve as a powerful tool to provide insights into the health, status, and overall performance of your projects. This section will walk you through what Project

Dashboards are, why they matter, how to set them up effectively, and best practices for using them to drive your team's success.

What Are Project Dashboards in Asana?

At its core, a **Project Dashboard** in Asana is a **visual reporting tool** that aggregates project data into easy-to-read **charts, graphs, and metrics**. Rather than digging through individual tasks or multiple projects, a dashboard gives you a **high-level overview** — showing you where things stand, highlighting bottlenecks, and pointing out trends that require your attention.

Dashboards allow you to:

- **Visualize key metrics** like task completion rates, overdue tasks, upcoming deadlines, and more.
- **Track multiple projects** and portfolios at once.
- **Create customized views** to focus on what's most important to your goals.

Asana's dashboards are dynamic, meaning they update automatically as your team works, providing you with real-time data without requiring manual updates.

Why Project Dashboards Matter

A project dashboard is more than just a pretty graph — it's a tool for better decision-making.
Here's why they are critical:

- **Clarity and Focus**: Dashboards offer a snapshot of the project's health, helping teams focus on priorities.
- **Accountability**: By making progress transparent, dashboards encourage team members to stay on track.
- **Early Problem Detection**: Spotting delays, overloaded team members, or resource constraints early allows you to course-correct before problems escalate.
- **Data-Driven Management**: With concrete data at your fingertips, you can move from intuition-based management to fact-based decision-making.

- **Stakeholder Communication**: Easily share progress with executives or clients without manually preparing reports.

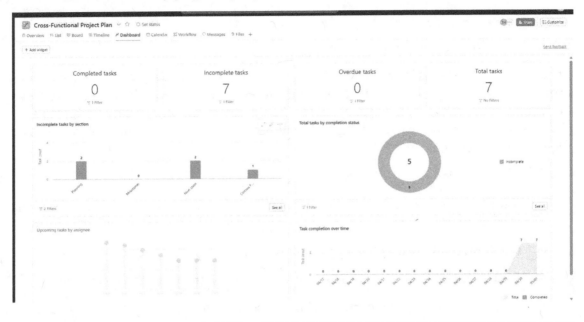

Components of an Asana Project Dashboard

When you create a dashboard in Asana, you have a range of **widgets** to build a complete picture of your project's status. Some of the main components you can include are:

1. Task Completion Charts

- Show how many tasks are complete, incomplete, or overdue.
- Track progress over time.

2. Burnup and Burndown Charts

- Burnup charts show the total work completed versus the total work planned.
- Burndown charts show how much work remains over time.

3. Task Count by Assignee

- See workload distribution among team members.

- Quickly identify if someone is overloaded.

4. Milestone Progress

- Visualize how far along the team is in achieving major goals.

5. Custom Field Breakdown

- Analyze data according to your custom fields (such as task priority, stage, or client).

6. Status Updates

- Attach regular status updates to keep a running log of project health.

How to Create a Project Dashboard in Asana

Setting up a dashboard is straightforward but being intentional about what you track is key. Here's a step-by-step process:

Step 1: Access the Dashboard Tab

1. Open the specific project you want to monitor.

2. Navigate to the **Dashboard** tab, found next to the "Overview" and "Messages" tabs.

Step 2: Add Charts and Widgets

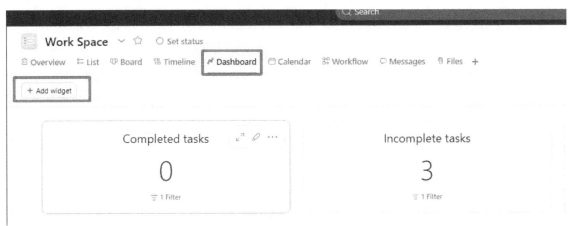

1. Click **"Add Chart"**.

2. Choose from different chart types:

- o Bar Charts

- o Line Charts

- o Pie Charts

- o Number Cards

3. Configure the chart:

   - o **Data Source**: Choose from tasks, milestones, assignees, or custom fields.

   - o **Filters**: Apply filters (e.g., only incomplete tasks, only tasks due this month).

   - o **Grouping**: Group data by fields like status, assignee, priority.

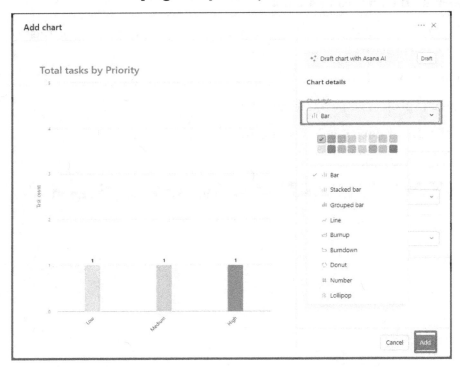

Step 3: Customize the Layout

- Arrange your charts for easy scanning.

- Focus on the most critical information at the top.

- Avoid overcrowding the dashboard; focus on 5–8 key metrics.

Step 4: Share Your Dashboard

- You can share project dashboards with your team or external stakeholders.
- Use the **Overview page** to share status updates linked to your dashboard metrics.

Tips for Building Effective Dashboards

Building dashboards is as much an art as a science. Here are some best practices:

1. Define Your Audience

- If the dashboard is for executives, focus on high-level outcomes.
- If it's for your internal team, you may want more operational details.

2. Keep It Simple

- Highlight the most critical information only.
- Too many widgets can overwhelm and dilute important insights.

3. Update Regularly

- While dashboards auto-update, your interpretation of the data should evolve.
- Update your status narratives and adjust widgets if your project focus changes.

4. Align Charts with Project Goals

- Every chart should serve a purpose aligned with project success metrics.
- Avoid adding charts just because the data is available.

5. Use Color Strategically

- Use Asana's color-coded fields and sections to draw attention where necessary.
- Green for "on track," Yellow for "at risk," Red for "off track."

Common Dashboard Use Cases

Here are examples of how different teams might use project dashboards in Asana:

Team	Common Dashboard Focus
Marketing	Campaign timelines, content production stages
Product	Sprint progress, feature completion rates
Sales	Lead tracking, deal stage movements
HR	Hiring pipeline, onboarding tasks
Operations	Process compliance, cross-team initiatives

Advanced Dashboard Features

If you're using Asana's Business or Enterprise plans, you gain access to **even more powerful features**:

1. Portfolios

- Create dashboards not just for one project but across multiple projects.
- Great for department heads managing many initiatives.

2. Advanced Reporting

- Create complex, cross-project reports.
- Aggregate data from different workstreams into a single view.

3. Goals Integration

- Link projects to organizational goals.
- Track project impact against high-level company OKRs.

Common Challenges and How to Overcome Them

Challenge	Solution
Dashboard is too cluttered	Focus on a few core metrics
Charts show misleading data	Double-check your filters and groupings
Team not using dashboard regularly	Integrate dashboard reviews into meetings
Hard to interpret data	Add explanations in your status updates

Summary

Project Dashboards in Asana are indispensable tools for visual project tracking. They make it easier to stay aligned, anticipate risks, and communicate effectively with your team and stakeholders. By carefully crafting your dashboard with intention — focusing on key metrics, updating regularly, and tailoring it to your audience — you transform project data into powerful insights that drive results.

Learning to master dashboards will not only keep your projects on track but also elevate your project management skills significantly. Whether you're managing a small internal project or leading a complex, cross-functional initiative, dashboards ensure you always have a clear view of the road ahead.

CHAPTER III
Building Custom Workflows

3.1 Introduction to Workflow Design

3.1.1 What Makes a Good Workflow?

When it comes to managing work effectively, **the design of your workflow is everything**. A good workflow acts like a well-paved road: it directs the flow of work clearly and efficiently, removing obstacles, minimizing confusion, and ensuring that all members of a team know exactly what to do, when to do it, and how their work fits into the bigger picture. In this section, we'll explore the key characteristics of an effective workflow, the common pitfalls to avoid, and practical steps to help you design workflows in Asana that truly drive results.

What Is a Workflow?

At its core, a workflow is a **sequence of steps** that a team or an individual follows to complete a piece of work. In the context of Asana, a workflow can range from a simple checklist for publishing a blog post to a complex series of interdependent tasks involving multiple departments launching a new product.

Every workflow answers the essential questions:

- What needs to be done?
- Who is responsible?
- When should it be done?
- How does one step lead into another?

Without a well-defined workflow, projects often suffer from delays, miscommunication, duplicated efforts, and missed opportunities.

Characteristics of a Good Workflow

A good workflow in Asana—or any project management system—shares several important traits:

1. Clarity

Clarity is non-negotiable. Every task within your workflow should have:

- A clear objective.

- A defined owner (assignee).

- A specific deadline or timeline.

Clear workflows prevent misunderstandings and reduce the need for constant clarifications. In Asana, this means ensuring that **every task and subtask is labeled properly**, assigned to the right person, and placed logically within the broader project structure.

Tip: Use Asana's "Task Descriptions" to clearly outline what is expected for each task.

2. Simplicity

Complexity can kill productivity. A good workflow is **as simple as possible**, while still capturing all necessary steps. Overcomplicating your process with unnecessary approvals, meetings, or tasks will bog down your team.

In Asana, you can keep things simple by:

- Using templates for common projects.

- Grouping related tasks with sections or columns.

- Avoiding excessive nesting of subtasks.

Pro Tip: Only add subtasks when absolutely necessary. Too many nested levels can confuse team members.

3. Logical Sequencing

Tasks should **flow naturally from one to the next**. Dependencies should be set where appropriate so that people know when they can start their work. In Asana, you can link tasks by marking them as **"dependent"** on the completion of other tasks.

For example:

- You can't start designing a website page until the copy has been written.

- You can't launch a product until testing is complete.

By using Asana's dependency feature, you ensure that team members get automatic updates when it's their turn to act.

4. Flexibility

No matter how well you plan, **things change**. Good workflows are **flexible** enough to adapt to changes in scope, deadlines, or resources.

In Asana:

- You can drag-and-drop tasks to adjust schedules.

- Easily reassign work as team members' availability changes.

- Add or remove steps without breaking the entire project.

Building flexibility into your workflows ensures resilience when unexpected challenges arise.

5. Accountability

Accountability is built into good workflows by **assigning ownership**. Each task should have **one clearly designated person responsible**. Even if multiple people are involved, there should be a single point of accountability.

In Asana:

- Assign tasks to individuals, not groups.

- Use the "Comment" feature for collaboration, but make sure each action item is directly assigned.

6. Visibility and Transparency

Team members should be able to **see the overall progress** and **understand where they fit in**. Asana offers features like dashboards, status updates, and progress bars to give everyone insight into project health.

Transparency helps:

- Identify bottlenecks early.

- Motivate teams as they see progress toward milestones.

- Foster trust among collaborators.

Insight: Regularly update project status in Asana using the "Progress" tab to keep all stakeholders informed.

7. Measurability

Finally, a good workflow must have **metrics for success**. You should define what success looks like at the beginning and track progress toward those goals.

In Asana, you can use:

- Goals to track key deliverables.

- Custom fields to monitor specific KPIs (e.g., budget, time spent).

- Reporting features to review completion rates, overdue tasks, and workloads.

Common Pitfalls in Workflow Design

Avoiding mistakes is just as important as following best practices. Common errors when designing workflows include:

- **Overcomplicating simple processes** with too many steps.

- **Failing to define task ownership**, leading to work falling through the cracks.

- **Ignoring dependencies**, causing team members to start work prematurely or wait unnecessarily.

- **Not building in review stages**, resulting in quality issues.

- **Lack of flexibility**, making it hard to pivot when needed.

Recognizing these pitfalls early ensures that your workflows remain efficient and effective over time.

Designing Your Workflow in Asana: Step-by-Step

Here's a simple process for designing an excellent workflow in Asana:

Step 1: Map Out Your Process on Paper First

Before jumping into Asana, outline your process. Use simple flowcharts or lists to visualize:

- Start points.
- Task sequences.
- Decision points.
- End goals.

This will prevent you from building a disorganized project structure inside Asana.

Step 2: Create a Project in Asana

- Choose between **List view** or **Board view** depending on the nature of your work.
- Give your project a clear, descriptive name.

Example: "Website Redesign Launch" or "New Hire Onboarding Process."

Step 3: Add Tasks and Structure

- Create tasks for each major action item.
- Use sections to group related tasks.

- Add subtasks sparingly for multi-step activities.

Step 4: Set Responsibilities and Deadlines

- Assign each task to a specific person.
- Set realistic due dates.
- Use Asana's "Priority" custom fields if necessary.

Step 5: Link Dependencies

- Identify which tasks rely on others.
- Set up dependencies using Asana's "Mark as Dependent" feature.

Step 6: Add Automations Where Possible

Use Asana's built-in Rules to:

- Move tasks automatically when marked complete.
- Notify team members when assigned.
- Adjust priorities based on task properties.

Step 7: Review and Test the Workflow

- Walk through the workflow step-by-step.
- Make adjustments where things feel clunky or confusing.
- Involve your team in testing before going live.

Final Thoughts

Designing a great workflow is both an art and a science. With Asana's tools and a strong understanding of what makes a workflow effective—**clarity, simplicity, logical**

sequencing, flexibility, accountability, visibility, and measurability—you'll be able to build systems that not only deliver results but also empower your team to do their best work.

In the next sections, we'll dive deeper into how to **automate** your workflows and **customize** them further using Asana's advanced features.

☑ **Up next: 3.2 Automating Workflows in Asana**

3.1.2 Mapping Out Your Process

In order to build a truly effective workflow in Asana, you need to first **map out your process** clearly. Mapping out your process helps you **visualize the sequence of work**, **identify bottlenecks**, **define roles**, and **establish a smooth flow of tasks**. A well-mapped process ensures that Asana doesn't just act as a simple task list, but as a dynamic and powerful system that mirrors how your team actually works.

In this section, we will walk through everything you need to know about **mapping out a workflow**, including why it's important, how to approach it, common mistakes to avoid, and step-by-step instructions to create your own workflow diagram before setting it up in Asana.

Why Mapping Your Process Matters

Before diving into Asana's tools and features, you need clarity on your actual work process. Without a mapped process, it's easy to create a disorganized Asana project that confuses team members instead of empowering them.

Here's why mapping is critical:

- **Clarity**: Everyone understands what steps are needed to complete work.

- **Efficiency**: Reduces wasted time caused by miscommunication or rework.

- **Accountability**: Assigns responsibilities to individuals or teams.

- **Scalability**: Makes it easier to onboard new team members or adjust the process as your organization grows.

- **Optimization**: Highlights inefficiencies or missing steps that you can fix before building your Asana project.

In short, a mapped process lays the foundation for building a perfect Asana workflow.

Key Principles of Workflow Mapping

When designing your process, keep the following principles in mind:

- **Simplicity**: Make the steps clear and avoid unnecessary complexity.

- **Consistency**: Ensure that each task or stage follows predictable rules.

- **Visibility**: Make sure the workflow is easily understandable by all participants.

- **Flexibility**: Allow room for changes and improvements over time.

Think of a workflow map as a **living document**. It should be updated regularly as you discover better ways of working.

Common Types of Workflows

Before mapping, it helps to know that workflows usually fall into one of the following categories:

- **Sequential Workflow**: Tasks happen one after another in a specific order. Example: A content article moves from writing → editing → design → publishing.

- **Parallel Workflow**: Multiple tasks can happen simultaneously. Example: Marketing and legal teams review a product announcement at the same time.

- **Conditional Workflow**: Different paths occur based on certain conditions. Example: If a feature passes testing, it moves to deployment; if not, it returns to development.

You can mix these types within the same project, depending on complexity.

Step-by-Step Guide to Mapping Out Your Process

Here's how to map out your process before building it in Asana:

Step 1: Identify the Goal

Start by answering: **What is the final output or goal of this workflow?**

For example:

- Delivering a new software feature
- Publishing a marketing campaign
- Organizing an event

Clearly defining the goal helps you reverse-engineer the necessary steps.

Step 2: List All Major Steps

Break down the work into major stages. Think about:

- What happens first?
- What happens next?
- What must happen before something else can start?

Write down each major step in plain language without worrying about Asana yet.

Example for a blog post workflow:

- Topic ideation
- Content draft
- Editorial review
- Graphic design
- Final approval
- Publishing

Step 3: Define Sub-Steps if Necessary

Some major steps may require several smaller tasks. Identify these sub-tasks now.

For example, "Content draft" might involve:

- Research
- Writing
- Internal peer review

Being granular helps later when assigning subtasks in Asana.

Step 4: Assign Roles and Responsibilities

For each step and sub-step, define:

- **Who is responsible for completing it?**
- **Who needs to be informed?**
- **Who needs to approve it?**

This ensures that tasks don't fall through the cracks.

Tip: Follow the **RACI Model** (Responsible, Accountable, Consulted, Informed) if your process involves multiple stakeholders.

Step 5: Identify Dependencies

Understand task relationships:

- **Which tasks must be completed before others can start?**
- **Are there tasks that can happen in parallel?**

In Asana, you will later use **dependencies** to build these relationships visually.

Step 6: Choose Tools and Deliverables

Decide what deliverables or outputs are expected from each stage.

Examples:

- A completed draft document
- A design file
- An approved proposal

Also, think about any tools or integrations needed (e.g., Google Docs, Dropbox, Slack).

Step 7: Visualize the Workflow

Create a simple diagram of your process using:

- A flowchart

- A whiteboard drawing

- A simple bulleted list

Tools like **Lucidchart**, **Miro**, or even Asana's own Boards view can help you create a rough sketch of your workflow.

A basic diagram for a blog post workflow might look like this:

Idea Submitted → Content Draft → Editorial Review → Design Creation → Final Approval → Publish Post

Step 8: Validate with Your Team

Before setting up the workflow in Asana, **review it with your team**.

Ask questions like:

- Is anything missing?

- Is the order logical?

- Are the responsibilities clear?

Adjust your process map based on feedback. It's better to fix problems at the mapping stage than during live execution.

Tips for Mapping Complex Workflows

For complex projects (e.g., software development, product launches), workflows may become intricate. Here's how to manage them:

- **Break Big Projects into Phases**: Use milestones to separate stages.

- **Create Separate Sub-Workflows**: For different departments or teams.

- **Use Conditional Paths**: If a step has different outcomes, map both paths.

- **Limit Overlaps**: Too many simultaneous tasks can cause confusion.

- **Document Decisions**: Write down why you chose certain paths for future reference.

Real-World Example: Mapping an Event Planning Workflow

Imagine you are planning a corporate event. Here's how you could map the process:

Goal: Host a successful annual conference.

Major Steps:

- Initial Planning
- Venue Booking
- Speaker Coordination
- Marketing and Promotion
- Logistics and On-Site Setup
- Event Execution
- Post-Event Follow-up

Sub-Steps Example (for Venue Booking):

- Research potential venues
- Request proposals
- Compare costs
- Visit top venues
- Sign contract

Roles:

- Event Manager (Responsible)
- Marketing Manager (Consulted)
- Finance Team (Informed)

Dependencies:

- Venue must be booked before marketing materials can be finalized.

- Speakers must be confirmed before agenda is created.

Deliverables:

- Signed venue contract

- Speaker list

- Marketing campaign materials

Workflow Visualization:

Initial Planning → Venue Booking → Speaker Coordination → Marketing Launch

↓

Logistics Preparation

↓

Event Day Execution

↓

Post-Event Reports

Once this mapping is complete, building it in Asana becomes straightforward: projects, tasks, sections, milestones, and dependencies naturally follow from this map.

Conclusion

Mapping out your process is not just an optional step — it's the **blueprint** that defines whether your workflow will succeed or fail in Asana.

By carefully defining the goal, major steps, sub-steps, roles, dependencies, and deliverables, you create a process that is **organized, scalable, and easy to execute**.

Once your workflow map is ready, you can move confidently into **building the workflow structure inside Asana**, ensuring that your digital setup perfectly mirrors the way your team works in reality.

In the next sections, we'll dive into how to **automate** parts of your workflow inside Asana, turning your map into a powerful, efficient system.

3.2 Automating Workflows in Asana

3.2.1 Creating Rules and Triggers

Automation is one of Asana's most powerful features, helping users streamline repetitive tasks, reduce manual effort, and ensure consistent processes across teams. In this section, we will dive deep into how to **create Rules and Triggers** in Asana, enabling you to automate your workflows and focus on the work that matters most.

Understanding Rules and Triggers in Asana

At its core, a **Rule** in Asana is a predefined automation consisting of a **Trigger** (the event that starts the Rule) and an **Action** (the result that happens after the trigger event). In simple terms: **"When X happens, automatically do Y."**

Rules help automate routine steps like assigning tasks, updating fields, moving tasks between sections, or sending notifications. This saves you time, ensures consistency, and reduces human error.

Example:

- **Trigger:** A task is marked complete.

- **Action:** Move the task to the "Completed" section and notify the project owner.

Benefits of Using Rules and Triggers

- **Efficiency:** Reduce manual work so you can focus on high-impact tasks.

- **Consistency:** Ensure processes are followed every time without deviation.

- **Visibility:** Automatically update team members on important changes.

- **Accuracy:** Eliminate errors caused by forgetting small process steps.

- **Scalability:** As your projects grow, automation helps you maintain structure without extra overhead.

Key Components of a Rule

Before we build one, it's important to understand the two main parts:

1. **Trigger:** What event happens to start the Rule? Example triggers:
   - Task is moved to a specific section
   - Task is marked complete
   - Due date is approaching
   - Priority is changed

2. **Action:** What should happen automatically after the trigger event? Example actions:
   - Assign the task to someone
   - Move the task to a new section
   - Update a custom field
   - Send a notification to a teammate

How to Create a Rule in Asana

Let's walk step-by-step through the process:

Step 1: Open Your Project

Navigate to the project where you want to set up a Rule. Only project owners, admins, or members with editing rights can create Rules.

Step 2: Access the Rules Panel

In the project toolbar at the top, you'll see a **Customize** button (sometimes shown as a magic wand icon). Click it, and scroll down to the **Rules** section. You'll find two options:

- Browse pre-made Rule templates
- Create a custom Rule from scratch

Step 3: Choose to Create a Custom Rule

Click **"Add Rule"** → **"Create Custom Rule"**.

This opens the Rule builder where you define:

- A **Trigger** (the event)
- One or multiple **Actions** (the consequences)

Step 4: Set the Trigger

You will be presented with various trigger categories, such as:

- Task changes (e.g., marked complete, due date changed)
- Field updates (e.g., priority changes)
- Comments added
- Attachments added

Select the appropriate trigger for your process.

Example:
Trigger: "Task moved to section 'Ready for Review'."

Step 5: Define the Action

Once the trigger is set, choose what action Asana should perform. You can pick multiple actions if needed.

Possible actions include:

- Assign task to specific teammate
- Add task to another project
- Change the due date
- Set a custom field value
- Post a comment on the task

Example:
Action: "Assign the task to the Quality Assurance Lead."

Step 6: Name Your Rule

Give your Rule a clear, descriptive name. Example: **"Auto-assign QA Review"** This helps you and your teammates understand what the Rule does at a glance.

Step 7: Save and Activate

Click **"Create Rule"** or **"Save"**, and your automation will go live! You can edit, deactivate, or delete the Rule anytime from the Rules panel.

Popular Use Cases for Rules and Triggers

If you're wondering where to start, here are some common automations you can quickly implement:

- **Task Handoff:** When a task moves to a "Ready for Review" section, automatically assign it to the reviewer.

- **Status Updates:** When a task is marked complete, move it to the "Completed" section and post a congratulatory comment.

- **Priority Management:** If the priority field is set to "High," automatically notify the team lead.

- **Recurring Meetings:** Automatically create a duplicate task every week for team stand-up meetings.

- **Deadline Reminders:** Send a reminder two days before a task's due date.

Advanced Rule Building: Multi-Step Automations

Asana allows Rules to trigger **multiple actions**. For example:

- When a task is moved to "Client Review":
  - Assign it to the Client Manager
  - Change the task's custom field "Status" to "In Review"
  - Add a comment: "Please review this task before the deadline."

Multi-action Rules make workflows even more efficient and ensure that all necessary steps are completed without manual intervention.

Understanding Limits and Best Practices

While Rules are powerful, there are some important things to know:

- **Rule Limits:** Some plans (especially Free plans) have a limited number of Rules. Premium and Business plans unlock more automation options.

- **Performance Impact:** Too many Rules firing at once can slightly slow down task updates. Keep automation clean and purposeful.

- **Clarity Matters:** Always name Rules descriptively so everyone knows their purpose.

- **Avoid Conflicting Rules:** Make sure Rules don't create loops (e.g., Task moves → triggers another Rule → moves back → triggers first Rule again).

Real-World Example: Automating a Marketing Campaign Workflow

Imagine you're running a marketing campaign in Asana. Here's how you could set up automation:

- **Trigger:** Task moves to "Ready to Publish"
- **Actions:**
    - Assign the task to the Publishing Team
    - Change the custom field "Campaign Status" to "Publishing"
    - Post a comment tagging the Publishing Lead
    - Add the task to the "Published Content" project

This ensures that as soon as a campaign is ready, the publishing process kicks off automatically — no more chasing people manually.

Troubleshooting Automation Issues

If a Rule doesn't work as expected:

- Double-check that both Trigger and Action conditions are set correctly.

- Ensure the Rule is activated (it will show "Active" next to it).

- Verify that the people or fields involved still exist (e.g., if someone left the team, an assign action may fail).

- Review Asana's activity log on the task to see if the automation attempted to fire.

Summary: Bringing Automation into Your Workflow

Using Rules and Triggers in Asana will revolutionize how you manage work. Instead of spending precious hours moving tasks, chasing updates, or manually updating fields, you can automate these steps with just a few clicks.

By mastering this feature, you'll not only boost your personal productivity but also create a more reliable, scalable, and high-performing team workflow.

Key Takeaways:

- Always start simple: build one Rule, test it, then layer complexity.

- Communicate with your team about new automations to avoid confusion.

- Review your automation setup regularly as your processes evolve.

Remember, automation isn't about replacing people — it's about empowering them to do their best work without getting bogged down by repetitive tasks.

3.2.2 Using Forms to Capture Work Requests

In the realm of project management, efficient intake of work requests is paramount. Asana Forms offer a streamlined solution, enabling teams to collect standardized information and automatically generate tasks within projects. This section delves into the creation, customization, and optimization of Asana Forms to enhance your workflow.

Understanding Asana Forms

Asana Forms are integrated tools that allow users to submit structured information, which is then transformed into tasks within a designated project. This feature is instrumental in standardizing work requests, ensuring that teams receive all necessary details upfront.

Key Benefits:

- **Standardization:** Ensures uniformity in the information collected.

- **Automation:** Automatically creates tasks upon form submission.

- **Accessibility:** Forms can be shared with both internal team members and external stakeholders.

Creating a Form in Asana

Step 1: Access the Project

Navigate to the project where you want the form submissions to appear.

Step 2: Open the Customize Menu

On the right-hand side of the project interface, click on the **Customize** button.

Step 3: Add a Form

Scroll down in the Customize menu and click on **+ Add Form**. This action will open the form builder interface.

Customizing Your Form

Form Title and Description:

Provide a clear title and a concise description to inform users about the purpose of the form.

Adding Questions:

Click on **+ Add Question** to include various fields. Asana supports multiple question types:

- **Short Text:** For brief responses.

- **Paragraph Text:** For detailed inputs.

- **Dropdown:** Allows selection from predefined options.

- **Radio Buttons:** Single-choice selection.

- **Checkboxes:** Multiple-choice selection.

- **Date:** For selecting dates.

- **Attachment:** Users can upload files.

Marking Required Fields:

Ensure essential information is captured by marking specific questions as required.

Linking to Custom Fields:

If your project utilizes custom fields, you can link form questions to these fields, allowing responses to populate directly into the task's custom fields.

Sharing the Form

Access Settings:

Determine who can access the form:

- **Anyone with the Link:** Ideal for external stakeholders.

- **Organization Members Only:** Restricts access to internal team members.

Distributing the Form:

Once configured, click on **Copy Link** to share the form via email, embed it on a website, or integrate it into other communication channels.

Product request

Name *

Enter your name

Email address *

Enter your email address

Active plan *

Choose one... ⌄

Product(s) *

☐ Jar

☐ Vase

☐ Bottle

☐ Box

Submit

Never submit passwords through Asana Forms.
Report abuse or check out our privacy policy.

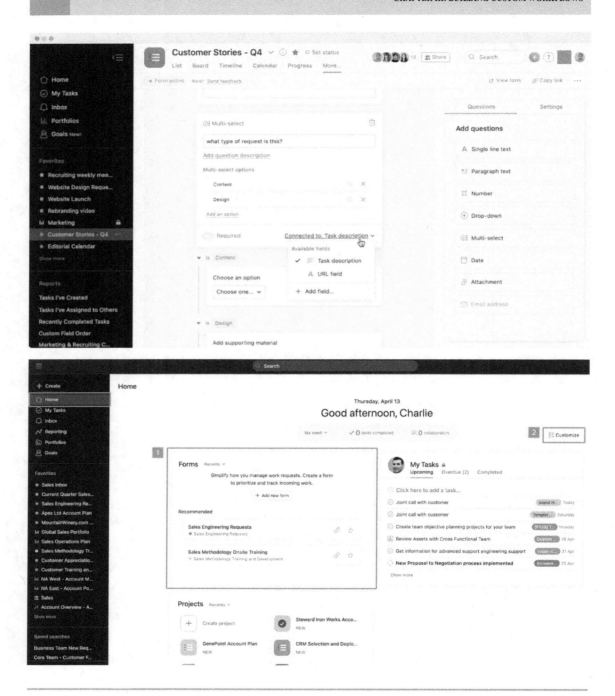

Managing Form Submissions

Each form submission automatically generates a task within the associated project. These tasks can be managed like any other, including assigning to team members, setting due dates, and adding to sections.

Automating Task Management:

Leverage Asana's Rules feature to automate actions upon form submission:

- **Assign Tasks:** Automatically assign tasks to specific team members.

- **Set Due Dates:** Establish default deadlines.

- **Add to Sections:** Organize tasks into appropriate project sections.

Best Practices for Using Asana Forms

- **Clarity:** Ensure questions are straightforward to avoid confusion.

- **Brevity:** Keep the form concise to encourage completion.

- **Testing:** Submit test entries to verify the form functions as intended.

- **Feedback:** Solicit feedback from users to refine the form over time.

Conclusion

Asana Forms are powerful tools for capturing work requests efficiently. By standardizing the intake process, automating task creation, and integrating seamlessly with your projects, forms can significantly enhance your team's productivity and clarity.

3.2.3 Setting Up Recurring Tasks

Recurring tasks are a vital component of any workflow that involves routine actions. Whether it's a weekly team meeting, monthly report submission, daily task check-ins, or regular status updates, recurring tasks allow you to automate repetitive responsibilities, ensure consistency, and maintain accountability—all without having to manually recreate the same task over and over again.

In this section, you'll learn how to set up, manage, and optimize recurring tasks in Asana to build a more efficient and scalable workflow.

Understanding Recurring Tasks in Asana

A recurring task in Asana is a task that automatically reappears at a set interval after completion. This function is particularly useful in workflows that have time-based consistency, such as:

- Weekly content publishing
- Monthly invoicing
- Daily standup reminders
- Quarterly performance reviews

Asana's recurring task function is flexible and supports a wide range of recurrence patterns. You can set a task to repeat daily, weekly, monthly, yearly, or on a custom schedule (like "every 2 weeks on Friday").

How Recurring Tasks Work

Here's how it works:

- A task is created and assigned a due date.
- You set the recurrence pattern using the task's due date menu.
- Once the task is marked as complete, Asana automatically generates the next occurrence based on the defined frequency.
- Each new instance carries over task details, assignees, attachments, and custom field values.

It's important to note: **the recurrence is triggered upon completion** of the current task. This ensures the system doesn't create duplicates prematurely and keeps the workflow clean.

Step-by-Step: Creating a Recurring Task

Let's walk through the exact steps to create a recurring task in Asana:

Step 1: Create a New Task

You can create a new task in any project or your "My Tasks" section.

1. Click the **+ Add Task** button.

2. Give your task a clear, actionable title (e.g., "Weekly Marketing Report").

3. Add any relevant details such as description, subtasks, assignees, attachments, and tags.

Step 2: Assign a Due Date

To schedule recurrence, you must first assign the task a due date.

1. Click on the **calendar icon** next to the due date field.

2. Select the initial due date for the first occurrence of the task.

Step 3: Set Recurrence

After setting the due date, click the **"Set to repeat"** option located in the due date popup.

You will then see several recurrence options:

- **Daily**: Repeats every day.

- **Weekly**: Repeats every week on the selected day(s).

- **Monthly**: Repeats every month on a specific date.

- **Yearly**: Repeats once a year on the selected date.

- **Periodically**: Custom intervals (e.g., every 2 weeks, every 3 months).

- **Custom Recurrence**: Offers the most control, allowing for complex schedules (e.g., every Monday and Thursday, or every 15th of the month).

Step 4: Confirm and Save

Once the recurrence schedule is set, confirm the task details and click **Enter** or **Save**.

The task is now configured to repeat upon completion.

Recurring Subtasks: How to Handle Them

It's important to know that **Asana does not automatically make subtasks recur** unless you set each one individually.

If your recurring task includes multiple subtasks (e.g., a checklist), and you want them to repeat each time the parent task recurs:

- Create the parent task with subtasks.

- Set the recurrence at the **parent task** level.

- When the parent task is completed, Asana will duplicate it **along with** its subtasks in their original state (e.g., unchecked, unassigned).

Note: If you set recurrence on **individual subtasks**, it may lead to multiple copies of subtasks, which can get messy. Therefore, apply recurrence at the **parent task** level for a cleaner setup.

Managing and Editing Recurring Tasks

To view or change recurrence settings:

1. Open the task.

2. Click the due date.

3. Edit the recurrence schedule as needed.

You can also **stop** recurrence at any time:

- Open the task → click on the due date → click **"Repeat"** → choose **"Never"**.

Changes made to the recurrence settings will apply only to the **future occurrences**, not those already completed.

Best Practices for Recurring Tasks

To get the most out of recurring tasks in Asana, consider the following practices:

1. Use Clear and Consistent Naming

Avoid vague titles like "Weekly Review". Instead, specify the purpose: "Weekly Team Performance Review – Marketing"

2. Use Custom Fields for Status Tracking

Add custom fields such as "Status" or "Priority" to recurring tasks so you can filter and monitor recurring task performance over time.

3. Automate Further with Rules

Combine recurring tasks with **Asana Rules** for enhanced automation. For example:

- When a new task is created, automatically assign it to a teammate.

- When a task is moved to a section, automatically set a due date.

4. Avoid Creating Recurring Tasks Too Far in Advance

Since each new instance is only generated **after completion**, you avoid cluttering your calendar or project with future tasks.

5. Include Instructions or Templates

If the recurring task has a fixed structure (e.g., weekly report), include a short template or checklist inside the task description.

Common Use Cases for Recurring Tasks

Here are a few real-world examples of recurring tasks in various industries:

Marketing

- Weekly content publishing schedule

- Monthly campaign review

- Quarterly competitor analysis

Operations

- Daily stock checks

- Monthly vendor audits

- Weekly supply ordering

HR

- Weekly 1:1 meetings
- Monthly payroll processing
- Annual performance evaluations

Software Development

- Daily standups
- Sprint planning every two weeks
- Biweekly code review reminders

Freelancers/Individuals

- Daily time tracking log
- Weekly client updates
- Monthly invoice sending

Troubleshooting Recurring Tasks

1. Task Doesn't Repeat After Completion

Make sure recurrence was properly set before completion. If recurrence is missing or incorrectly configured, the task won't duplicate.

2. Task Duplicates With Errors

Double-check task templates to ensure there are no conflicting rules or automation that modify recurring task structure upon duplication.

3. Subtasks Not Carrying Over

Asana will copy subtasks with the parent task only if the recurrence is set at the parent level. If you need recurring subtasks independently, set recurrence individually for each.

Alternatives to Recurring Tasks

In some situations, recurring tasks may not be the ideal solution. You may consider alternatives such as:

- **Templates**: For workflows requiring manual customization, reusable task or project templates might be more flexible.

- **Forms**: Combine forms with automation to trigger task creation upon request submission.

- **Recurring Events in Google Calendar** (if integrated with Asana): Use calendar reminders when precise scheduling is more important than task duplication.

Final Thoughts

Recurring tasks are a simple yet powerful feature in Asana that can bring structure, rhythm, and automation to your workflow. By leveraging recurring tasks properly, you reduce manual work, increase accountability, and ensure important tasks never slip through the cracks.

Start small by identifying one or two repetitive responsibilities and turn them into recurring tasks. Over time, as you become more comfortable, you'll be able to build robust routines that support your team's productivity at scale.

3.3 Advanced Features for Workflow Customization

3.3.1 Custom Fields

Asana is a powerful work management tool, but what truly unlocks its potential is its ability to adapt to your specific workflow. One of the most essential features that enables this level of customization is **Custom Fields**. Whether you're managing a simple content calendar or a complex product launch, Custom Fields help you track critical information beyond just task titles and due dates.

In this section, we'll explore what Custom Fields are, how to create and manage them, and the best practices for integrating them into your workflows for maximum efficiency and visibility.

What Are Custom Fields in Asana?

Custom Fields in Asana allow users to add structured data to tasks. Unlike standard fields (e.g., assignee, due date, tags), Custom Fields are user-defined and can be tailored to reflect any relevant attribute of a task or project. Think of them as the "columns" in a spreadsheet that you design to match your work style.

For example, you could create:

- A **priority field** with options like High, Medium, and Low.

- A **stage field** for tracking progress: To Do, In Progress, Review, Completed.

- A **budget field** to input numerical values.

- A **department field** using dropdown options for cross-functional projects.

These fields can appear across projects and allow teams to **standardize data**, **filter views**, **sort tasks**, and **create reports** based on criteria that matter most to them.

Types of Custom Fields

Asana currently supports several types of Custom Fields. Each field type is designed for a particular kind of data and interaction.

1. Dropdown Fields

- Let users select from a predefined list of options.
- Useful for categories like status, priority, departments, or roles.
- Each option can be color-coded for better visibility.

2. Text Fields

- Provide open text input for flexible information.
- Great for notes, internal codes, or short comments.
- Not ideal for structured filtering but helpful for reference.

3. Number Fields

- Designed for numeric data (e.g., hours, costs, quantities).
- Allow for sorting and calculations in dashboards.
- Often used in time tracking, budgeting, or effort estimation.

4. Date Fields *(Available in some tiers)*

- Store additional date values beyond the standard due date.
- Useful for fields like launch date, review date, etc.

Creating Custom Fields

Creating a Custom Field in Asana is straightforward and intuitive.

Step-by-Step: Adding a Custom Field to a Project

1. **Open the desired project** in Asana.
2. Click on the **"Customize"** button (top right).
3. Scroll to the **"Fields"** section and click **"+ Add field."**
4. Choose to either:

- o **Create a new field**, or

- o **Reuse an existing field** from your organization's field library.

5. Select the **field type**: Dropdown, Text, or Number.

6. Enter a **field name**, optional description, and (for dropdowns) the values and colors.

7. Click **"Create Field."** It will now appear on all tasks in the project.

Field Library and Reusability

Asana encourages consistency through a **Field Library** (available for Premium and above workspaces). When you create a Custom Field, you can choose to make it available across other projects. This is especially helpful for fields like "Priority" or "Status" that are relevant in multiple teams.

Benefits of using the Field Library:

- Keeps naming and options consistent across departments.

- Enables **Portfolio views** and **Reports** to function cohesively.

- Simplifies onboarding for new users.

Managing and Editing Custom Fields

Editing a Custom Field

- Click on the field header in the project.

- Select the pencil icon to rename, add/edit options, or change colors.

- Updates to global fields reflect in all projects using them.

Deleting a Custom Field

- From the "Customize" menu, click the three-dot menu next to the field.

- Select "Remove from project" (does not delete the field globally).

- To permanently delete a global field, go to the **Admin Console** (for admins only).

Using Custom Fields in Workflows

Custom Fields become incredibly powerful when incorporated into your project workflows. Here are ways they can transform how your team works:

1. Task Organization

- Group and sort tasks by priority, department, or phase.

- Use fields to visually separate work types in board and list views.

2. Reporting and Dashboards

- Custom Fields feed into **advanced search filters**.

- They enable the use of **Charts** and **Dashboards** (in Portfolios).

- Example: Create a chart showing tasks by status, or total budget by department.

3. Workflow Automation

- Combine Custom Fields with **Rules** (Asana automation).

  o Example: If Priority is "High," then assign to a team lead.

  o If "Status" is changed to "In Review," automatically notify reviewers.

4. Approval Processes

- Create a dropdown field like "Approval Status" with values such as Pending, Approved, Rejected.

- Combine with rules to trigger updates or notifications.

5. Multi-Team Coordination

- Use fields like "Owning Department" or "Client Name" across teams.

- Streamline cross-functional work by filtering or reporting based on these shared values.

Best Practices for Using Custom Fields

To get the most from Custom Fields, consider these best practices:

☑ Keep Fields Standardized

Avoid creating too many similar fields (e.g., "Priority Level", "Priority", "Task Urgency"). Use your organization's Field Library to maintain consistency.

☑ Use Clear Naming Conventions

Name fields and values in a way that all team members understand. Avoid abbreviations unless they're widely known internally.

☑ Limit the Number of Fields

Too many fields can clutter your interface. Only use what is necessary for decision-making and tracking.

☑ Review and Update Fields Regularly

As workflows evolve, Custom Fields may become obsolete or require new options. Schedule periodic reviews.

☑ Combine with Templates

If you use the same fields repeatedly, integrate them into **project templates** to save time and enforce standardization.

Examples of Effective Custom Field Setups

Marketing Campaign Tracker

- Campaign Type (Dropdown)

- Stage (Dropdown: Planning, Live, Post-Mortem)

- Budget (Number)

- Launch Date (Date)

Product Development Workflow

- Feature Type (Dropdown: UI, Backend, Bug Fix)

- Priority (Dropdown: Low, Medium, High)

- Estimated Effort (Number: Hours)
- Status (Dropdown: Backlog, In Progress, QA, Done)

Client Onboarding Process

- Client Name (Text)
- Onboarding Stage (Dropdown)
- Onboarding Owner (Dropdown or Assignee)
- Start Date / Completion Date (Date)

Common Pitfalls to Avoid

- **Redundancy:** Don't create a new field every time a similar need arises.
- **Over-complication:** Avoid using complex fields that slow down users.
- **Inconsistent usage:** Train team members on what each field means and how to use it correctly.

How Custom Fields Fit into the Bigger Picture

Custom Fields are not isolated—they work hand-in-hand with nearly every Asana feature:

- They power **Rules, Templates, Reports, Portfolios**, and **Workload tracking**.
- When thoughtfully implemented, they act as the **data backbone** of your project operations.
- They bridge the gap between task management and organizational visibility.

Conclusion

Custom Fields are one of the most flexible and valuable features in Asana's toolbox. By tailoring your projects to track what matters most, you enhance clarity, foster accountability, and empower better decision-making.

They provide a structured way to organize, prioritize, automate, and report on your team's work—transforming Asana from a simple task manager into a full-fledged workflow engine.

In the next section, we'll dive even deeper into these capabilities with a look at **Task Dependencies**—another advanced feature that enables smart, sequential work and keeps your team aligned.

3.3.2 Task Dependencies

In any project management system, understanding the relationship between tasks is vital for successful execution. Asana's **Task Dependencies** feature allows teams to define and visualize how one task relies on the completion of another, making it easier to manage priorities, avoid bottlenecks, and improve workflow efficiency.

This section will dive deep into what task dependencies are, how to use them in Asana, best practices for managing dependent tasks, and real-world examples to help you fully leverage this advanced feature in your daily operations.

What Are Task Dependencies in Asana?

At its core, a task dependency is a relationship between two tasks where one task (the "dependent" task) cannot begin until another task (the "blocking" task) has been completed. This creates a sequential structure to your project, ensuring that tasks are tackled in the correct order.

In Asana, this is expressed by linking two tasks together using the "Mark as dependent" function. Once a dependency is established, Asana will automatically notify assignees when the blocking task has been completed, allowing them to proceed with their work without delay.

For example:

- **Task A**: "Write blog draft"
- **Task B**: "Edit blog post" (dependent on Task A)

This means Task B cannot start until Task A is finished.

Why Use Task Dependencies?

Using task dependencies enhances project clarity and control. Here are several compelling reasons to use this feature:

- ☑ **Improves Planning Accuracy**: Helps ensure tasks are sequenced correctly.

- ☑ **Prevents Overlaps and Bottlenecks**: Ensures no one starts work before the prerequisite is complete.

- ☑ **Clarifies Team Responsibilities**: Assignees know exactly when they can start.

- ☑ **Boosts Transparency**: Everyone on the team sees how tasks are interconnected.

- ☑ **Enhances Automation**: Dependencies can be used in combination with Rules to automate follow-up steps.

How to Add Task Dependencies in Asana

Step-by-Step Guide (Web and Desktop App)

1. **Open the Task You Want to Make Dependent** Navigate to the task detail pane of the task you want to set as dependent.

2. **Click on the "Dependencies" Icon** Look for the chain-link icon labeled **"Add dependencies"** or "Mark as dependent".

3. **Select the Blocking Task** Choose the task that must be completed first (the one this task is waiting on).

4. **View Dependency Link** Once linked, you will see a note stating: "Waiting on [Task Name]". The blocking task will also display: "[Task Name] is waiting on this task."

Using Timeline View for Dependencies

Timeline view is ideal for setting and managing task dependencies visually:

- Drag from one task to another to create a dependency link.

- You can adjust task start and end dates to reflect changes in timeline automatically.

- Asana highlights any dependency conflicts, such as a dependent task being scheduled before its predecessor.

Types of Dependencies in Asana

Asana supports **Finish-to-Start** dependencies (task B starts after task A is finished). While this is the most common form of dependency, teams can mimic more complex relationships through naming conventions, rules, and custom fields.

Other types you may simulate manually:

- **Start-to-Start**: Two tasks start simultaneously.

- **Finish-to-Finish**: Two tasks end at the same time.

- **Start-to-Finish**: Rare, but where one task can't end until another begins.

Currently, Asana natively supports only Finish-to-Start but integrations and thoughtful structuring can emulate the others.

Managing Dependencies at Scale

Managing dozens or even hundreds of dependencies can become complex in large projects. Here's how to stay on top:

1. Use Timeline View Effectively

- Adjust task dates to reflect changes.

- Watch for overlapping tasks or scheduling conflicts.

- Collapse or expand project sections for better visibility.

2. Use Portfolios and Goals (Advanced Plans)

- Monitor cross-project dependencies and progress.

- Spot risks early when milestones across multiple teams are interconnected.

3. Use Automation Rules

- Set rules like: "When a task is no longer waiting on another → mark it as Ready to Start."

- Create status updates that are triggered by completed dependencies.

4. Set Clear Task Ownership

- Assign every task to one owner.

- Use comments or custom fields to clarify who should begin work once the blocker is resolved.

Notifications and Alerts for Dependencies

Asana is designed to keep everyone informed when a dependent task becomes unblocked:

- The assignee of the dependent task gets a notification that they can begin.

- The "waiting on" message disappears from the task pane.

- You can also set up rules to assign or move tasks automatically once the blocking task is completed.

This reduces the need for constant status check-ins, improving team productivity.

Common Pitfalls and How to Avoid Them

Pitfall	How to Avoid
Creating circular dependencies (A depends on B, B depends on A)	Always double-check logic when linking tasks.
Forgetting to update dependencies when rescheduling	Use Timeline view and adjust dependencies as you shift dates.
Overusing dependencies on trivial tasks	Only set dependencies where delays truly affect workflow.
Not communicating dependency changes	Keep stakeholders informed, especially when using dependencies across teams.

Best Practices for Task Dependencies

Here are some best practices to help you get the most out of task dependencies in Asana:

- **Plan before you build**: Map out your full workflow before assigning dependencies.

- **Use dependency visualizations**: Leverage Timeline view for a clear view of what's connected.

- **Avoid overcomplication**: Not every task needs a dependency; use them purposefully.

- **Combine with custom fields**: Use "Status" or "Blocked/Unblocked" fields to enhance visibility.

- **Automate where possible**: Use rules to notify or reassign tasks as dependencies are resolved.

Real-World Use Cases

Marketing Campaign Launch

- Task: "Write email copy" → Task: "Design email" → Task: "Schedule email"
- Dependencies ensure design doesn't start until copy is approved.

Product Development

- Task: "Finish frontend UI" → Task: "Integrate backend API" → Task: "User testing"
- Dependency chain ensures code is tested in the right order.

Client Onboarding Process

- Task: "Sign agreement" → Task: "Set up account" → Task: "Kickoff meeting"
- Guarantees key steps happen in the correct sequence.

Using Integrations with Dependencies

Some tools enhance dependency management:

- **Zapier**: Trigger actions in other apps when dependencies are completed.

- **Slack Integration**: Alert team channels when a blocker is resolved.

- **Google Calendar Integration**: Visualize dependency-driven timelines on personal calendars.

Future Potential: What Could Come Next

While Asana already handles dependencies well, here's what users are hoping for in future updates:

- Multiple dependency types (e.g., Start-to-Start)
- Automated critical path detection
- Gantt-style optimization suggestions
- AI-based workload rebalancing based on dependencies

Stay tuned to Asana's product updates and forum to discover new enhancements as they roll out.

Summary

Task dependencies in Asana are a powerful way to structure complex workflows, reduce delays, and increase visibility across your projects. By using them effectively, you can ensure that work flows logically from one step to the next, enabling teams to focus on what matters most — delivering results.

In this section, you've learned:

- What task dependencies are and how to create them
- How to manage and visualize them using Asana tools
- Common pitfalls to avoid
- Best practices for leveraging dependencies across teams
- Real-world applications that demonstrate their value

When used thoughtfully, task dependencies transform Asana from a basic task manager into a dynamic project engine.

3.3.3 Portfolios and Goals

In the realm of project and task management, being able to zoom out and see the big picture is just as important as being able to manage the individual components. That's where **Asana's Portfolios and Goals** come in—two of the most powerful tools for executives, team leads, and cross-functional managers who need visibility into overall strategy, progress, and performance.

This section will guide you through what Portfolios and Goals are, how to set them up, and how to use them to align daily work with broader strategic initiatives. We'll also walk through best practices, use cases, and common pitfalls to avoid.

What Are Portfolios and Goals in Asana?

Portfolios

Portfolios in Asana are a way to group multiple projects together so you can monitor them all in one place. Each portfolio serves as a **real-time status dashboard**, giving you instant visibility into the progress, health, and priority of multiple projects at once. Portfolios are especially useful for team leads managing several initiatives or department heads tracking programs across teams.

Goals

Goals are Asana's built-in objective-setting feature. They allow you to define **strategic objectives**, link them to specific projects or tasks, and track progress over time. Think of Goals as a layer above Portfolios—while Portfolios track the execution, Goals define **what success looks like**.

Together, Portfolios and Goals enable **strategic alignment**, allowing teams to execute work that's both coordinated and clearly tied to outcomes that matter.

Setting Up a Portfolio

Creating a Portfolio is straightforward, but setting it up thoughtfully can make a significant difference in how effectively you manage your projects.

Step 1: Navigate to Portfolios

To access Portfolios:

- Click on **"Portfolios"** in the sidebar (available for *Asana Business* and *Enterprise* plans).

- Alternatively, click the **"+" button** next to the Portfolios section and select **"Create Portfolio"**.

Step 2: Create a New Portfolio

Give your portfolio a name that reflects the group of projects it will monitor—for example:

- "Product Launches Q3"

- "Marketing Campaigns 2025"

- "Client Onboarding Projects"

You can also add a **description** that explains its purpose or the criteria for inclusion.

Step 3: Add Projects

Now, populate your portfolio by adding existing projects. You can:

- Search and select from your existing projects.

- Add projects owned by other team members (depending on permissions).

- Include cross-functional projects that contribute to the same objective.

Each added project will appear as a card showing:

- Project name

- Project owner

- Status (On Track, At Risk, Off Track, or Custom)

- Progress (% completion based on tasks completed)

- Due date

Step 4: Customize the View

You can sort and filter your Portfolio view by:

- Project owner

- Status

- Due date

- Progress percentage

Use **Custom Fields** to add even more context—e.g., Priority, Region, Budget, etc.

Tracking Project Health and Progress

Portfolios are more than a list—they are a **live control center**.

Project Status Updates

Project owners can submit **weekly or monthly status updates** from within their projects. These updates appear in the Portfolio view and usually include:

- A short summary of progress

- Key accomplishments

- Roadblocks or risks

- A status indicator (Green, Yellow, Red)

As a Portfolio owner, you can review all updates in one place and reach out proactively if something needs attention.

Progress Metrics

Each project in the portfolio shows a **progress bar** based on task completion. Asana calculates this automatically:

- Completed tasks / Total tasks = Progress %

This helps you see which projects are behind, on schedule, or ahead.

Timeline View in Portfolios

Asana's **Timeline View** in Portfolios lets you see the **start and end dates** of multiple projects side by side. This is extremely useful for:

- Capacity planning

- Avoiding overlapping timelines

- Identifying dependencies across projects

Creating and Managing Goals in Asana

Setting up Goals allows teams to **tie their daily work to strategic business outcomes**.

Step 1: Access Goals

Goals are located in the sidebar. Click **"Goals"** to view the organization's goal list, and then click **"Create Goal."**

Note: Goals are only available in *Business* and *Enterprise* plans.

Step 2: Define a Goal

When creating a Goal, you'll enter:

- **Name:** E.g., "Increase Website Traffic by 30%"
- **Owner:** The person responsible for achieving the goal
- **Collaborators:** Team members involved
- **Start and End Dates**
- **Progress Metric:** You can choose either:
    - **Milestone-based** (Manual progress tracking)
    - **Number-based** (e.g., go from 1000 → 1300 leads)
- **Description:** The context and criteria for success

You can also nest your Goal under a **parent goal** to show alignment with broader company objectives.

Step 3: Link Projects and Tasks

To make your Goal **actionable**, link it to:

- Projects that support the goal (e.g., "SEO Campaign – Q2")
- Individual tasks or subtasks that directly impact the outcome

This feature ensures **goal visibility** and **accountability**, as stakeholders can see the work tied to the goal in real time.

Monitoring and Reporting on Goals

Progress Updates

You can manually or automatically update goal progress. If linked to a numeric target (e.g., "revenue"), you can input actual figures as progress updates.

If tied to a project's progress (e.g., task completion), the progress bar updates automatically.

Goal Hierarchy

Goals can be:

- **Company-wide**
- **Team-level**
- **Individual-level**

This cascading structure encourages alignment. For example:

- Company Goal: "Improve Customer Satisfaction by 15%"
  - Team Goal: "Reduce Support Response Time to Under 4 Hours"
    - Individual Goal: "Automate FAQ System"

Filtering and Views

You can filter Goals by:

- Status (On Track, At Risk, Off Track)
- Owner
- Timeframe
- Team

These views give leadership a **clear picture** of how the organization is progressing across initiatives.

Best Practices for Using Portfolios and Goals

1. **Keep Portfolios Focused**: Avoid turning a Portfolio into a dumping ground for all projects. Group projects by common objective, function, or timeframe.

2. **Use Consistent Status Updates**: Encourage project owners to submit updates on the same schedule. This enables easier cross-project comparison.

3. **Align Goals with Measurable Outcomes**: Ensure every goal has a clear, quantifiable target. Avoid vague goals like "Improve Collaboration"—instead say "Increase Cross-Team Project Delivery by 20%."

4. **Link, Don't Duplicate**: Use Asana's linking features to connect tasks, projects, and goals rather than creating redundant copies.

5. **Review Goals Regularly**: Treat goal review as a living process. Check on progress at least monthly, and adjust strategies as needed.

Use Cases: Real-World Scenarios

Marketing Campaign Oversight

A marketing manager uses a Portfolio to track all campaigns and their statuses. Goals are set quarterly for leads generated, and each campaign project is tied to that goal.

Product Development Coordination

A product team leader creates a Portfolio for all feature development projects. Goals are linked to OKRs (Objectives and Key Results) such as "Launch 3 Core Features by Q4."

Executive Dashboard

A COO has Portfolios by department and can check on delivery timelines, health, and blockers in one glance. Goals help track annual targets like revenue or customer retention.

Common Pitfalls to Avoid

- **Not Using Progress Metrics Consistently**: Inconsistent use of fields like "status" or lack of updates defeats the purpose of centralized visibility.

- **Creating Too Many Goals**: Limit active goals to what can realistically be tracked and achieved. Overloading the system with low-impact goals reduces focus.

- **Poorly Defined Project Boundaries**: If projects within Portfolios don't have clear scopes, it becomes difficult to track real progress.

Conclusion

Portfolios and Goals in Asana are your bridge between **strategic vision** and **tactical execution**. Whether you're overseeing product rollouts, managing multiple client projects, or aligning teams to quarterly objectives, these features ensure that every task contributes to a larger outcome. By setting up clear portfolios, defining actionable goals, and maintaining disciplined tracking, you empower your teams to work with purpose, clarity, and momentum.

When used effectively, Portfolios and Goals transform Asana from a task management tool into a **strategic operating system for your organization**.

CHAPTER IV
Collaborating with Your Team

4.1 Communicating in Asana

4.1.1 Commenting and Mentions

Effective communication is the heartbeat of any successful team project. In a collaborative workspace like Asana, the goal isn't just to complete tasks—it's to ensure every team member is informed, aligned, and empowered to act. Asana integrates communication directly into the context of your tasks, allowing conversations to happen exactly where work is being tracked. This is where *comments* and *mentions* come into play—two simple but powerful tools that transform how teams coordinate and communicate.

The Role of Comments in Asana

Unlike traditional email threads or chat apps that live outside the work itself, Asana comments are embedded directly within tasks, subtasks, and project updates. This contextual messaging system means that every discussion happens where it matters most—alongside the work being done.

Types of Comments in Asana:

1. **Task Comments:** These appear in the activity feed of a specific task. Team members use them to:

   o   Clarify instructions

   o   Ask questions

   o   Share updates

   o   Link to relevant documents or resources

   o   Give feedback

2. **Subtask Comments:** Like task comments, these are specific to a subtask and often used in more detailed conversations, especially when a task has multiple moving parts.

3. **Project Status Comments:** Used during project status updates, these comments help team leads provide high-level insight and solicit feedback from stakeholders.

4. **Inbox Comments:** Although not comments per se, Asana's inbox consolidates all comment activity so users can quickly respond and stay in the loop.

How to Leave a Comment

Leaving a comment is simple but knowing how to use it effectively is essential.

Steps:

1. Open a task or subtask.

2. Scroll to the bottom of the task pane.

3. Type your message in the comment box.

4. (Optional) Use @mention to tag someone directly.

5. Click **Comment** or press Enter.

Comment Formatting Tips:

- Use **line breaks** (Shift+Enter) for readability.

- Use emojis to humanize digital conversation ☺ .

- Be concise but clear—remember that others may revisit the comment days or weeks later.

- For important information, consider bolding key terms or using bullet points.

The Power of Mentions

Mentions are created using the @ symbol and can reference:

- People

- Tasks

- Projects

- Teams

- Custom fields (in some cases)

Mentions transform static comments into dynamic tools by directly notifying the mentioned user or linking to the referenced item.

Example:

"Hey @Jordan, can you upload the Q2 financial report here? Also, see task @#112345 for context."

Use Cases:

- **Tagging someone for action:** "@Linh, can you review this by Friday?"

- **Referencing related work:** "Please coordinate this with @Launch Plan."

- **Encouraging collaboration:** "Let's discuss this in the @Marketing Team channel."

- **Creating traceability:** "The client feedback is already listed in task @Client Meeting Notes."

Mentions generate notifications, prompting real-time engagement while keeping everything documented.

Best Practices for Using Comments and Mentions

1. Keep It Action-Oriented

When writing comments, especially those requesting action, use clear verbs and mention deadlines. Example:

"@Alex, please finalize the copy edits by Thursday so we can move to design."

2. Avoid Redundancy

Don't repeat comments across multiple tasks. Instead, use mentions to link relevant discussions and avoid fragmented conversations.

3. Respect Notification Overload

Mention only those who are truly involved. Over-mentioning can lead to disengagement.

4. Use Mentions to Pull in Stakeholders

If someone is not assigned but should be aware, mention them in a comment rather than assigning the task. This keeps roles clean while ensuring visibility.

5. Update Comments Rather Than Starting New Threads

If your update is a direct response to an earlier discussion, reply within the same thread rather than starting anew. This improves continuity.

Collaborating Across Time Zones with Comments

For distributed teams, asynchronous collaboration is vital. Comments and mentions help bridge the time gap. When one team member leaves a detailed comment, others can pick up the thread later without needing real-time communication.

Tips for asynchronous comment collaboration:

- Leave context: Don't assume prior knowledge.

- Attach files or screenshots for visual clarity.

- Timestamp deadlines: "Due by EOD Friday (GMT+7)"

Comment Notifications and the Asana Inbox

When you're mentioned in a comment or someone replies to a thread you're part of, Asana notifies you in the **Inbox** (in-app) and optionally via **email or mobile push notification**.

Managing Comment Notifications:

- Users can unfollow a task if notifications become excessive.

- You can set Asana notification preferences under **My Settings > Notifications**.

This flexibility ensures you stay informed without being overwhelmed.

Real-World Scenarios

Case Study 1: Creative Team Collaboration

A designer uploads a draft to a task and comments:

"@Ella, here's the first version of the brochure. Feedback appreciated!"

Ella replies:

"Love the layout! Can you make the font size 14pt? Also, @George, can you double-check the product specs?"

This fluid exchange keeps everything within the task, creates a documented feedback loop, and eliminates the need for an external email thread.

Case Study 2: IT Support Request

An internal support task reads:

"@IT Team, laptop for new hire @Linda needs setup by Friday."

As each action is completed, comments update progress. Mentions ensure relevant team members are looped in without ambiguity.

Pitfalls to Avoid

- **Using comments as a chat substitute:** Asana comments are powerful, but for real-time or casual conversation, use integrated tools like Slack.

- **Too many mentions:** Not every update needs to ping multiple users.

- **Assuming visibility:** Just because a comment is posted doesn't mean it's seen. When in doubt, mention.

- **Burying information in long threads:** If something is critical, summarize it at the top of the task description or pin the comment.

Leveraging Comments for Team Culture

Comments can also be a space for positive reinforcement. Saying "Great job!" or adding a 🎉 emoji can go a long way in building morale, especially in remote teams.

Use for:

- Celebrating milestones
- Encouraging teammates
- Recognizing effort

Summary: Why Comments and Mentions Matter

Comments and mentions in Asana are not just about exchanging messages—they're about **embedding communication into the workflow itself**. This leads to:

- Fewer meetings
- Clearer accountability
- Better project traceability
- Higher productivity

Used effectively, these tools turn Asana from a static task list into a dynamic collaboration platform.

4.1.2 Sharing Files and Resources

Effective collaboration requires more than just assigning tasks—it demands clear, timely access to the information and assets your team needs to succeed. Asana streamlines file and resource sharing within projects and tasks, creating a centralized workspace where documentation, media, and links are always just a click away. This section explores how you can use Asana to attach, manage, and organize files and resources for seamless team collaboration.

Why File Sharing Matters in Collaborative Work

In traditional project management setups, files are often scattered across multiple platforms—email threads, cloud folders, and local drives—leading to lost time and miscommunication. With Asana, files and documents are directly tied to the tasks and projects they support, so your team always knows where to find what they need.

The ability to easily access resources—project briefs, mockups, spreadsheets, reports, presentations, and more—within Asana contributes to:

- **Clarity:** Everyone sees the most up-to-date version of a file.

- **Efficiency:** Files are available in the exact context where they're needed.

- **Accountability:** Teams understand how resources relate to task completion.

- **Transparency:** Stakeholders stay informed without needing to request updates or documents.

Attaching Files to Tasks

Every Asana task can house supporting files, creating a digital "file cabinet" for specific work items. To attach a file:

1. **Open a Task** – Click on any task in your project.

2. **Click the Attachment Icon (Paperclip)** – You'll see this in the task toolbar or comment box.

3. **Choose Your File Source:**

   o Upload from your computer.

   o Attach from cloud services: Google Drive, Dropbox, OneDrive, or Box.

   o Paste a link (e.g., Figma, Notion, YouTube, SharePoint).

Files attached in this way appear within the task details, making them visible to all collaborators with access to the task.

Best Practices:

- **Name files clearly.** Use consistent file naming conventions.

- **Attach the latest version only.** Avoid confusion by removing or replacing outdated versions.

- **Use the description field for context.** Provide a brief explanation of what the file is and how it should be used.

Attaching Files in Comments

Sometimes you need to share a resource during a conversation. Asana allows you to attach files directly within task comments.

- Start a comment.
- Click the attachment icon.
- Choose your file.
- Post your comment.

This method is useful for sharing feedback or updates related to specific files. The file becomes part of the task's comment history and is time-stamped with your input.

File Integrations: Leveraging Cloud Storage

Asana integrates natively with popular cloud storage providers, allowing teams to link and preview files without leaving Asana.

Supported Integrations:

- **Google Drive** – Add Docs, Sheets, Slides, PDFs, and more.
- **Dropbox** – Attach any file stored in your Dropbox account.
- **OneDrive** – Link Word documents, Excel spreadsheets, PowerPoint files, etc.
- **Box** – Secure file access with enterprise-grade features.

These integrations are particularly powerful because:

- You don't have to upload files—they're linked directly.
- Any updates to the original file are reflected automatically.
- Permissions are maintained as per the cloud platform's rules.

💡 **Tip:** When using cloud links, make sure your team has the necessary access rights. Sharing settings on the external platform (e.g., Google Drive) control who can view or edit.

Attaching Files to Projects

While most file sharing happens at the task level, you can also attach files to entire **projects**—ideal for documentation that applies to all tasks within a project.

1. Open the project.

2. Go to the **Overview** tab.

3. Scroll to the **Key Resources** section.

4. Click **Add Resource** and choose from:

   o File Upload

   o Link (URL)

   o Existing task or milestone

Project-wide files may include:

- Project plans and charters

- Branding guidelines

- Timelines and Gantt charts

- Team handbooks

Organizing Shared Resources

As projects grow, so do the number of files. To stay organized:

Use Sections and Subtasks to Structure Work

Break down tasks with attached files into logical categories. For example, in a design project:

- **Main Task:** Final Logo Design

  o Subtask 1: Initial Sketches (attach image files)

  o Subtask 2: Client Feedback Round 1 (attach annotated PDF)

  o Subtask 3: Final Revisions (attach Illustrator file)

Label Resources with Custom Fields or Tags

If you use **Custom Fields**, you can mark whether a task includes:

- Draft

- Final Version

- Needs Review

You can also use **Tags** like "Client Review," "Internal Use," or "Approved."

Pin Critical Files

In the project's **Overview** tab, pin your most critical resources using the "Key Resources" feature so they stay visible and accessible to the team.

Previewing and Viewing Files in Asana

When you attach files to Asana from supported platforms, you can often **preview** them directly within the app:

- Images and PDFs can be previewed in full-screen.

- Google Docs, Sheets, and Slides open in a pop-up window.

- Links to platforms like Figma or Loom may generate embedded previews.

This allows you to quickly check content without downloading or switching tools.

Version Control and File Updates

While Asana is not a full version control system, it can support lightweight version tracking through clear file naming and communication.

Here's how:

- Add version numbers to file names (e.g., Proposal_v1.2.pdf).

- Comment when uploading a new version with a brief explanation.

- Use subtasks or custom fields to track approval stages (e.g., "Awaiting Feedback," "Approved").

To avoid confusion, always remove or hide outdated versions. Only link to the most recent file in the task description or comments.

Security and Access Control

Asana respects your file permissions, especially for cloud storage links. But there are a few things to keep in mind:

- **Files uploaded from your device** are visible to anyone with access to the task.
- **Files linked from Drive/Dropbox/etc.** obey the permissions set in those platforms.
- **Private Projects** and **Limited Access Members** can restrict who sees files.

To secure sensitive documents:

- Use project or task privacy settings.
- Set sharing restrictions in Google Drive/Dropbox to "View only."
- Avoid uploading confidential files directly—use cloud services with tighter control.

Using Asana Forms for Resource Collection

Another way to collect resources from collaborators or external stakeholders is by using **Asana Forms**. This feature allows anyone (even outside your organization) to submit files via a form that creates a task automatically.

Use cases:

- Client onboarding: Upload branding assets via form
- Bug reporting: Attach screenshots to report form
- Content requests: Submit briefs and examples

Steps:

1. Create a form in your Asana project.
2. Add a **File Upload** field.

3. Share the form link.

Submitted files will be attached to the task generated by the form—organized and instantly available.

Collaborating Around Shared Resources

Don't just attach files—**collaborate** on them:

*   Use comments to give feedback directly on tasks with files.

*   Mention specific teammates (@username) to alert them to changes.

*   Create follow-up tasks or subtasks based on file contents (e.g., revisions needed).

*   Set due dates and assignees to ensure file reviews stay on track.

Combining file sharing with Asana's core collaboration features turns documents into dynamic work assets—not just static references.

Common Mistakes and How to Avoid Them

Even in a streamlined system, mistakes can happen. Avoid the following:

Mistake	Solution
Attaching multiple conflicting file versions	Use clear naming and remove old versions
Forgetting to update cloud sharing permissions	Always double-check link settings
Uploading files without context	Include a description or comment to explain usage
Misplacing critical resources	Pin them in the project overview or key tasks
Sharing files in private tasks no one else can see	Check task privacy settings carefully

Summary: Making the Most of File Sharing in Asana

Sharing files and resources in Asana isn't just about attaching documents—it's about creating **clarity**, **collaboration**, and **context** for every piece of work your team delivers.

Whether you're managing marketing campaigns, product launches, or client services, ensuring the right people have the right files at the right time is essential.

By following best practices—centralizing files, linking cloud storage, organizing attachments meaningfully, and communicating around resources—you transform your Asana workspace into a true hub for collaborative execution.

4.1.3 Team Conversations and Messages

Effective communication is the heartbeat of successful collaboration, especially in the digital workplace where remote work, asynchronous schedules, and cross-functional teams are now the norm. Asana recognizes the need for seamless team communication and has built-in tools to foster clarity, alignment, and transparency. One of these is **Team Conversations and Messages** — features designed to replace endless email threads, fragmented chats, and misaligned updates.

In this section, we will explore how Team Conversations and Messages work in Asana, when and how to use them, best practices to keep communication clean and purposeful, and how they differ from comments on tasks or project updates.

What Are Team Conversations and Messages in Asana?

Team Conversations in Asana are threaded, topic-based discussions that are visible to all team members. They are not tied to a specific task or project, making them perfect for broader discussions like brainstorming, announcements, or policy updates.

Messages, on the other hand, allow you to send direct or group messages to teammates, specific people, or groups within the workspace. Think of them as Asana's alternative to internal emails or quick team memos — but with the added advantage of being trackable, linkable, and stored in one place.

Together, these tools serve two distinct communication purposes:

- **Conversations** = For broader, team-wide topics or general announcements.

- **Messages** = For more direct, action-oriented communication between users or select groups.

When to Use Conversations and Messages vs. Task Comments

Before diving into how to use these tools, it's essential to know **when** to use them:

Use Case	Tool to Use
Asking for clarification on a specific task	Task Comment
Sharing company-wide or team-wide policy updates	Team Conversation
Brainstorming ideas for an upcoming project	Team Conversation
Notifying a project lead about a project delay	Direct Message
Following up on a side discussion between two collaborators	Message
Providing feedback on design files linked to a task	Task Comment

Use the right tool at the right time to avoid confusion and keep information structured and accessible.

How to Start a Team Conversation

Here's a step-by-step guide to initiating a team conversation in Asana:

1. **Navigate to the Team Page**: On the left-hand sidebar, under "Teams," click on the team you want to communicate with.

2. **Select the 'Conversations' Tab**: Once in the team workspace, you'll see several tabs — "Projects," "Calendar," "Conversations," etc. Click on "Conversations."

3. **Start a New Conversation**: Click the "New Conversation" button. You'll see a simple editor where you can:

   o Add a **subject/title**

   o Write your **message content**

   o Attach files or add links

   o Mention teammates using **@mention**

   o Add tags or assign follow-up tasks directly

4. **Send Your Conversation**: Once sent, everyone in the team will be notified (depending on their notification settings), and the conversation becomes a part of your team's history — searchable and referenceable at any time.

Using Messages in Asana

If you need to reach out to specific individuals or small groups within your organization, use the **Messages** feature. Here's how:

1. **Open the Message Composer**:
   - You can click on a teammate's profile picture and choose "Send Message," or
   - Use the inbox or team page to compose a new message.

2. **Choose Recipients**:
   - You can message one person, multiple individuals, or an entire project team.

3. **Compose Your Message**: The editor supports formatting, attachments, links, and @mentions.

4. **Send and Track**: All sent messages appear in the recipient's Inbox, ensuring visibility and traceability.

Unlike conversations, messages are more private and don't appear on the team's public message board.

Best Practices for Team Conversations

To make the most of Team Conversations, consider these tips:

1. Be Clear and Concise

Just like any professional communication, your conversation subject line should accurately reflect the topic, and your message body should be well-structured with bullet points or subheadings if needed.

2. Keep It Purposeful

Avoid using conversations for banter or off-topic messages. Stay focused on team-relevant issues like planning, updates, feedback, or strategy discussions.

3. Use Mentions Strategically

Mentioning teammates ensures that the right people get notified. However, avoid over-tagging — only include those who truly need to respond or be aware.

4. Follow Up with Tasks

Asana allows you to create tasks directly from conversation replies. This is especially useful for turning ideas into action. If someone suggests an idea, click "Create Task" from their comment to track it.

5. Archive Old Conversations

While conversations are searchable, older ones can clutter your interface. Archiving unneeded threads helps keep your team's communication hub tidy.

Best Practices for Messages

Messages should be used intentionally and with consideration of your teammates' workload and communication preferences.

1. Avoid Message Overload

Asana is not a chat tool like Slack or Microsoft Teams. Use Messages for more thoughtful, structured communication rather than back-and-forth chatter.

2. Reference Tasks and Projects

Messages allow you to link to existing tasks or projects. This makes it easy for recipients to navigate to the topic of discussion and take action.

3. Use for Sensitive or Focused Discussions

If you're giving feedback, requesting performance updates, or discussing sensitive project issues, Messages are more appropriate than public Conversations.

Notifications and Inbox Integration

Both Messages and Conversations are tightly integrated with **Asana's Inbox**. Here's how it works:

- New messages or replies to conversations you're involved in show up in your Inbox.

- You can choose to **Follow** or **Unfollow** conversations based on relevance.

- Clicking on the Inbox item takes you straight to the thread.

- You can archive or mark messages as read to stay organized.

For teams that rely heavily on Asana as their central communication tool, inbox management becomes a critical skill. Encourage your team to regularly clear or manage their Asana inboxes to avoid missing important updates.

How Conversations and Messages Support Transparency and Culture

Asana Conversations help reinforce a culture of **transparency and shared knowledge**. When ideas and updates are shared publicly (within the team), everyone stays aligned. This eliminates the silo effect and ensures that decisions are visible and open for feedback.

Meanwhile, Messages provide a controlled channel for nuanced communication — enabling leaders, project managers, or team members to communicate clearly, directly, and thoughtfully.

In hybrid or remote environments, using Conversations and Messages strategically reduces miscommunication, helps onboard new team members faster (who can read past threads), and maintains a documented history of decisions and discussions.

Common Pitfalls to Avoid

1. **Using Conversations for Everything**: Not every discussion needs to be a full conversation. For quick notes, use task comments or messages instead.

2. **Failing to Respond**: Conversations only work when people participate. Set expectations around response time and engagement.

3. **Duplicate Threads**: Search before starting a new conversation. Duplicate threads fragment discussions and lead to confusion.

4. **Lack of Structure in Messages**: Messages that are too long or unclear get ignored. Use bullet points, bolding, or headers where possible.

Summary

Team Conversations and Messages are core communication features in Asana designed to replace cluttered email chains and disorganized team chats. While **Conversations** serve as a central board for team-wide updates and discussions, **Messages** allow for direct, controlled communication between individuals or groups.

Used well, these tools improve:

- Transparency
- Accountability
- Team alignment
- Productivity

By understanding when and how to use each, and by following best practices, teams can communicate more efficiently and stay on the same page — no matter where or how they work.

4.2 Managing Team Projects

4.2.1 Setting Permissions and Privacy

Effective collaboration in Asana doesn't just involve assigning tasks and adding comments — it also requires clear, structured permissions and privacy settings that align with your team's needs and your organization's security requirements. In this section, we will explore the different types of permissions available in Asana, how privacy controls work, and the best practices for managing who can see and interact with various projects, tasks, and teams.

Understanding Asana's Permission Hierarchy

Asana is designed to be flexible and user-friendly when it comes to managing access. At the core of this flexibility is a **hierarchical structure** of permissions that control visibility and actions across different levels of the platform. These levels are:

1. Organization/Workspace

2. Teams

3. Projects

4. Tasks

5. Custom Fields and Goals (Advanced Plans)

Let's break down what each level allows:

Organization/Workspace Level

- If you're using Asana with a company domain (e.g., john@company.com), you're in an **Organization**.

- All members using the same domain are automatically part of the same Organization.

- You can control who is a **Member** (with broader access) and who is a **Guest** (restricted to specific projects or teams).

- Admins (for Business and Enterprise plans) can manage global user access and security settings through the **Admin Console**.

Team Level

- Teams are groupings within an Organization — typically used for departments like Marketing, HR, or Product.

- Each team has its own privacy setting:

  - **Public to Organization**: Anyone in the Organization can see and join the team.

  - **Request to Join**: Members can ask to join, but approval is required.

  - **Private**: Only visible and accessible to members who are invited.

Project Level

- Projects can be **Public to the Team** or **Private to Project Members**.

- Public projects allow for open collaboration, while private ones are useful for sensitive initiatives (e.g., HR or leadership strategies).

- Admins or project owners can control who is added as a **Project Member**, and they can assign roles like:

  - **Editor**: Can add/edit/delete tasks and details.

  - **Commenter**: Can view and comment, but not make changes.

Task Level

- By default, if someone can view the project, they can view the tasks within it.

- However, **tasks can be made private** by removing them from public projects or assigning them only to individuals.

- You can also use **task followers** to notify specific individuals who need updates, without granting full editing access.

Setting Permissions for Different Use Cases

Let's explore some common team scenarios and how you might configure permissions and privacy settings in Asana.

1. Cross-Functional Projects (Marketing + Product + Sales)

Goal: Enable multiple departments to work on the same initiative (e.g., a product launch) without compromising sensitive data.

Best Practices:

- Create a **cross-functional team** in Asana (or use an existing one).

- Make the **project public to the team**, but **control task visibility** using assignees and private subtasks where needed.

- For shared files, use integrated tools like Google Drive with limited document permissions.

Who Should Have What Access:

- Project Managers: **Editor**

- Department Heads: **Editor or Commenter** (depending on involvement)

- Executive Sponsors: **Commenter**

2. Confidential HR Projects (Recruitment, Performance Reviews)

Goal: Restrict access to sensitive employee information.

Best Practices:

- Create a **private team** (e.g., "HR Only").

- Keep projects **private to project members**.

- Only add **Editors** who are directly working on the task or process.

Additional Tips:

- Use **form submissions** with restricted visibility for collecting sensitive info (e.g., candidate evaluations).

- Ensure that guests (external recruiters) are added only as **task followers or project commenters** when necessary.

---

3. Company-Wide OKRs or Goals

Goal: Provide visibility into high-level objectives while maintaining control over editing.

Best Practices:

- Create a project under a **public team**.

- Use **Portfolios and Goals** (Business/Enterprise tiers) for visual tracking.

- Assign only a few individuals as **Editors**, with others as **Commenters** to prevent accidental changes.

Working with Guests and External Collaborators

Guests in Asana are users **without your company's email domain**. They're often clients, freelancers, or contractors who need limited access.

What Guests Can Do:

- View only what they're invited to (projects, tasks, or teams).

- Cannot browse other parts of your organization.

- Can be Editors or Commenters within their limited access.

Best Practices for Guest Access:

- Create dedicated **client-facing projects** with restricted scope.

- Keep communication task-specific — use **task comments** instead of broader team conversations.

- Always review sharing settings before adding guests to prevent data leaks.

Managing Privacy and Permissions as an Admin

If you're an **Organization Admin** (available in Asana Business and Enterprise), you have access to powerful controls through the **Admin Console**:

Key Admin Features:

- **User management**: Add, suspend, or remove users.

- **Team settings**: Set team creation policies and default privacy levels.

- **Data control**: Export project data, audit access logs, and integrate security tools (Enterprise only).

- **Authentication options**: Enforce **Google SSO**, **SCIM provisioning**, or **two-factor authentication**.

Admins can also limit:

- Guest invitation rights

- App integrations per team

- Public team creation

How to Set Permissions in Practice

To Set Project Permissions:

1. Open the project.

2. Click on the **Share** button in the top right.

3. Add members and choose **Editor**, **Commenter**, or **Viewer** roles.

4. Adjust project visibility: **Public to Team** or **Private to Members**.

To Set Team Privacy:

1. Go to the team in the sidebar.

2. Click the three-dot menu > **Edit Team Settings**.

3. Choose from **Public**, **Request to Join**, or **Private**.

To Share a Task Privately:

1. Open the task.

2. Click on the **Share** button or task assignee box.

3. Add individuals or remove from any shared project to isolate it.

Common Mistakes and How to Avoid Them

Mistake 1: Adding Sensitive Info to Public Projects

- **Fix**: Create a new private project or isolate the task and share it only with essential stakeholders.

Mistake 2: Overloading Users with Editor Access

- **Fix**: Assign **Commenter** or **Viewer** roles unless editing is absolutely necessary.

Mistake 3: Inviting Guests to Entire Teams

- **Fix**: Only invite them to specific **projects or tasks**. Use guest permissions wisely.

Mistake 4: Not Reviewing Default Privacy Settings

- **Fix**: Periodically audit team and project visibility to ensure settings align with organizational goals.

Tips for Scaling Permissions in Large Organizations

For larger teams or organizations managing dozens of projects:

- **Standardize templates** with correct privacy and permission settings.

- Create a **team onboarding doc** explaining who gets what level of access and why.

- Use naming conventions to indicate access level (e.g., " 🔒 HR - Performance Reviews").

- Encourage project leads to review access quarterly and remove inactive collaborators.

Conclusion: Permissions as the Foundation of Trust and Efficiency

Permissions and privacy settings in Asana are more than just tools for control—they're foundational to **building trust**, ensuring **data security**, and enabling **productive collaboration**. When used wisely, these settings can help you scale your workflows without friction, invite the right stakeholders without risk, and ensure everyone feels confident about what they can access and contribute.

4.2.2 Managing Workloads

Introduction: Why Workload Management Matters

Effective workload management is the backbone of any successful team. Without visibility into who is doing what and when, even the most talented teams can become overwhelmed, misaligned, or underutilized. In Asana, managing workloads isn't just about task allocation—it's about ensuring your team has the capacity to deliver high-quality work on time, while also maintaining a sustainable pace.

The **Workload** feature in Asana (available in Premium plans and above) gives team leads and project managers a centralized view of team capacity. It allows for real-time adjustments, so you can prevent burnout, avoid bottlenecks, and ensure optimal productivity. In this section, we'll walk you through the entire process of using Workload in Asana—from setup to advanced strategies—to help you make informed resourcing decisions.

Understanding Workload in Asana

Before diving into how to use Workload, it's essential to understand how it works:

- **Workload View** is part of the **Portfolios** feature.
- It provides a timeline-based view that shows tasks assigned to each team member over a specified time range.
- It uses **effort-based metrics**—typically based on **Custom Fields** like estimated hours or points—to calculate workload.
- Tasks can be adjusted in this view to balance assignments across your team.

Key benefits include:

- Avoiding overloading team members

- Identifying underutilized resources

- Planning realistic timelines

- Ensuring task distribution matches skills and availability

Step-by-Step: Setting Up Workload Management

1. Create or Open a Portfolio

To access Workload, you need to use Asana's **Portfolio** feature.

1. Click on **Portfolios** in the left sidebar.

2. Create a new Portfolio (e.g., "Q2 Marketing Initiatives") or open an existing one.

3. Add projects to the Portfolio that are relevant to the team whose workload you want to manage.

2. Add and Configure Custom Fields for Effort Tracking

Workload calculations rely on numerical values to gauge the effort of each task. These values come from **Custom Fields**.

- Common effort metrics:

  o Estimated Hours

  o Points (Agile/Scrum teams)

  o Time Blocks (e.g., 0.25 for 15 minutes)

- Create a custom field by:

1. Opening a project.

2. Clicking **Customize > Add Field**.

3. Choose a number type field and name it (e.g., "Estimated Hours").

4. Apply this field across all relevant projects to ensure consistency.

3. Assign and Populate Custom Fields

Once the custom field is added:

- Go to each task and input the estimated value (e.g., 3 hours for writing a blog post).

- Encourage team members or project leads to fill this out during task creation or planning.

4. Open Workload View in the Portfolio

- Navigate back to your Portfolio.

- Click the **Workload** tab at the top.

- You will now see a timeline with each team member listed and bars representing their assigned tasks.

Tasks will display:

- Their start and due dates.

- Their effort value (if input correctly).

- A colored bar that shows how much load they carry during the given period.

Balancing Workloads in Real Time

In the Workload view, you can now **adjust workloads on the fly**.

Visual Cues

- **Overloaded team members** will have red bars indicating overcapacity.

- **Underloaded members** may appear in green or have minimal assignments.

Rescheduling Tasks

- Drag and drop tasks within the timeline to different dates.

- Adjust start and due dates to spread the workload more evenly.

Reassigning Tasks

- Hover over a task and click the assignee's name.

- Choose a different team member from the dropdown to shift responsibility.

Splitting Tasks

If one task has too much effort for one person, consider splitting it:

- Create a new subtask and assign it separately.

- Divide the estimated effort across the subtasks.

Using Workload Filters and Sorting

You can filter Workload views to enhance clarity:

- By project

- By role (e.g., all designers or writers)

- By Custom Field values (e.g., show only tasks over 8 hours)

You can also sort by:

- Task volume

- Effort

- Alphabetically (for easier scanning)

These filters help you focus on critical tasks or overburdened roles.

Integrating Time-Off and Availability

Asana allows you to mark team members as **unavailable** for certain days, such as PTO or holidays.

- Click on the person's name in the Workload view.

- Select the date(s) they will be unavailable.

- The system will automatically reflect this unavailability, reducing their total available effort for that period.

This is especially useful for planning around vacations, public holidays, or part-time schedules.

Real-World Use Cases

Marketing Teams

Use Workload to allocate time for campaign planning, content creation, design, and reporting. Avoid overwhelming designers during launch phases by spreading design tasks out over multiple weeks.

Product Development Teams

Balance developer assignments during sprint planning. Prevent one engineer from being assigned 30+ hours in a 40-hour workweek while others only have 10.

Agencies and Consultants

Use Workload to manage client projects across various account managers. Helps prevent overbooking and ensures equal distribution of billable hours.

Tips for Effective Workload Management

1. Review Weekly

Schedule a **weekly review** of the Workload view. Make it part of your sprint planning or weekly team check-in.

2. Update Effort Estimates Regularly

Encourage your team to revise effort fields as projects progress. What started as a 2-hour task might need 6 hours after new requirements are added.

3. Use Workload for Forecasting

Want to know whether your team can take on a new project next month? Use Workload to **forecast** based on current and planned tasks.

4. Train Team Members

Make sure your team understands how effort fields work, what the values mean, and how they impact visibility for everyone.

Common Pitfalls to Avoid

- **Not using consistent effort units:** Mixing hours with points across projects can distort data.

- **Missing task dates:** Tasks without due dates won't appear in Workload timelines.

- **Underreporting actual workload:** Encourage honest reporting—even small admin tasks count.

- **Micromanaging via workload:** Use it for visibility and support, not for control.

Beyond Basics: Workload + Portfolios + Goals

To take Workload to the next level:

- Link your workload views to **Goals** (available in Business plans) to see if capacity aligns with strategic objectives.

- Use **Project Status Updates** to reflect how workload impacts deadlines.

- Combine Workload insights with Portfolio metrics (like On Track or At Risk) to make data-driven decisions.

Final Thoughts

Workload management in Asana is a game-changer for any team that wants to maximize productivity without overburdening team members. When used properly, it enables better planning, healthier work-life balance, and higher-quality deliverables.

Remember: Workload isn't about watching over your team's shoulder—it's about providing support, foresight, and balance. By understanding how your people are allocated, you can lead more effectively, plan more strategically, and deliver work with greater confidence.

4.2.3 Tracking Team Performance

Introduction: Why Team Performance Matters

In a world where remote and hybrid teams are increasingly common, tracking team performance has become more critical than ever. Effective performance tracking helps managers identify bottlenecks, allocate resources efficiently, recognize top performers, and make informed strategic decisions. In Asana, team performance is not just about numbers—it's about visibility, accountability, and alignment with shared goals. This section explores how Asana's features can empower managers and team members alike to stay aligned, productive, and continually improving.

1. Understanding What "Performance" Means in Asana

Before diving into tools and metrics, it's essential to define what performance looks like in Asana. Unlike traditional employee evaluation systems, Asana's performance tracking focuses on **task and project-based metrics**, including:

- Task completion rates
- On-time delivery
- Milestone achievement
- Project progress updates
- Resource allocation and workload balance
- Team responsiveness and collaboration quality

Asana doesn't measure performance with subjective scores or KPIs directly. Instead, it provides **data-rich visualizations** and **activity logs** that offer insights into how work gets done and who is doing it.

2. Using Dashboards to Monitor Progress

One of the most powerful tools in Asana for tracking performance is the **Dashboard** feature, which is available in the **Premium** and **Business** plans.

Creating Custom Dashboards

Dashboards are visual summaries of project data. You can build dashboards using **custom charts and widgets**, such as:

- Tasks completed over time

- Overdue tasks per assignee

- Time to completion for specific task types

- Milestones achieved per project

Steps to create a dashboard:

1. Open any project.

2. Click the **"Dashboard"** tab at the top.

3. Use the **"+ Add Chart"** button to add data widgets.

4. Choose a metric (e.g., completed tasks), group by (e.g., assignee), and display style (e.g., bar, donut).

Insights from Dashboards

Dashboards provide quick overviews of:

- Who is completing the most/least work.

- What tasks are frequently delayed.

- How different teams or departments are performing.

- Whether overall project delivery is improving or slipping.

By reviewing these dashboards regularly, you can spot trends and intervene early when issues arise.

---

3. Leveraging Workload Views for Resource Management

If you're on Asana Business, the **Workload** view provides a bird's-eye view of how work is distributed across your team.

What the Workload View Shows

- A timeline-based layout that maps tasks by assignee and due date.

- Work effort (measured in custom units such as hours or points).

- Overloaded or underutilized team members.

- Task conflicts and overlapping assignments.

How to Set It Up

1. Go to a **Portfolio** that contains your projects.

2. Click the **Workload** tab.

3. Assign custom fields like "Estimated Effort" or "Time" to measure workload.

4. Adjust assignments to balance work across the team.

Managing Capacity and Burnout

By monitoring workload:

- You can reassign tasks to avoid burnout.

- You ensure no one is underutilized.

- You can make proactive staffing decisions based on real data.

Workload balancing is directly linked to performance. When team members are overwhelmed, quality and punctuality suffer. Conversely, balanced teams are more productive and engaged.

---

4. Milestones and Status Updates

Tracking performance isn't just about individual contributions; it also involves monitoring **project-wide momentum**.

Using Milestones to Track Key Deliverables

Milestones mark critical points in a project's timeline. In Asana:

- They appear visually on **Timeline** views.

- They are great for tracking project phases (e.g., "Design Complete", "Launch Approved").

Use milestones to:

- Monitor if your team is hitting major goals on schedule.

- Hold members accountable for phase-specific deliverables.

- Ensure cross-functional alignment.

Weekly or Bi-Weekly Status Updates

Project owners can post status updates summarizing:

- What's been done
- What's blocked
- What's next

This is a great way to maintain performance visibility and transparency. Updates can include:

- Charts from the Dashboard
- Recent milestones achieved
- Key upcoming deadlines

---

5. Activity Feed and Task History

Performance can also be reviewed on a **micro-level** using task-level history and activity feeds.

Task Activity Feed

Every task in Asana includes an **activity history** that logs:

- Who created the task
- When status or assignee changed
- When comments were added
- When attachments were uploaded

This allows managers and team leads to:

- Track accountability
- Review task progress
- See communication timelines

Exporting Activity for Review

Admins or Project Managers can also:

- Export task history to CSV

- Review past due dates and completion metrics

- Audit changes over time for performance evaluation

6. Integrating Performance Tools with Asana

You can expand Asana's native capabilities by connecting it with third-party performance tracking platforms:

Integration with Time-Tracking Tools

- Harvest, Toggl, Clockify: track actual time spent per task.

- Compare estimated vs. actual effort for performance metrics.

CRM and Sales Performance Metrics

- Integrate Asana with Salesforce, HubSpot, or Pipedrive.

- View sales team activity and task completion rates within Asana workflows.

Power BI and Google Data Studio

- Export Asana data into visual analytics dashboards.

- Build advanced performance reports filtered by time, project, team, or role.

7. Using Goals and OKRs

In Asana's **Goals** feature (available in Business and Enterprise tiers), you can:

- Create organization-wide or team-level goals

- Link projects and tasks to specific goals

- Track goal progress as tasks are completed

Examples:

- Goal: "Increase Product Launch Speed by 15%"
- Linked Tasks: Product tasks with due dates, measured delivery times

This system allows for outcome-based performance tracking rather than just output-based.

---

8. Setting Up a Performance Review Ritual in Asana

To foster a culture of performance improvement, consider building a recurring performance review process within Asana itself.

Create a Performance Review Project

- Sections: Monthly Reviews, Quarterly Reviews, Goals, Notes
- Tasks for each team member with self-assessment, manager notes, and peer feedback

Use Forms to Collect Feedback

- Create Asana Forms for anonymous or structured input from colleagues.

Analyze Trends Over Time

- Use past review data, dashboard metrics, and task history to spot growth and areas for improvement.

---

9. Encouraging Transparency and Recognition

Tracking performance isn't only for identifying problems—it's also for celebrating wins.

Recognize Top Performers

- Use comment threads, "@mention" in updates, and celebrations like Asana's confetti unicorns to highlight achievements.

Foster Open Dialogue

- Encourage open feedback through comments and conversation threads.
- Support underperforming team members with additional resources or training plans.

Conclusion: Turning Performance Tracking into Performance Growth

Asana gives teams the structure and visibility they need to operate efficiently. But performance tracking is only valuable if it leads to better outcomes. With dashboards, workload views, milestones, activity logs, and integrated tools, teams can move beyond guesswork and into data-driven, accountable performance management.

Key takeaways:

- Track both individual and team-level progress

- Use visual tools to monitor, balance, and report

- Align daily work with strategic goals

- Create systems that encourage ongoing feedback and improvement

By leveraging Asana to its full potential, managers become coaches, and teams become empowered units—aligned, productive, and motivated to succeed.

4.3 Best Practices for Team Collaboration

4.3.1 Establishing Communication Norms

Effective team collaboration doesn't just happen automatically—it is built on a foundation of clear, consistent, and intentional communication. In the context of Asana, where much of your team's interaction happens asynchronously through tasks, projects, comments, and messages, setting communication norms is vital to ensuring that collaboration remains productive and efficient rather than scattered or overwhelming.

This section will guide you through why communication norms matter in Asana, how to establish them, and specific best practices you can implement to improve your team's workflow and communication culture.

Why Communication Norms Matter in Asana

Asana is a powerful work management tool, but without agreed-upon norms around how it's used, it can become disorganized and even counterproductive. Here's why communication norms are essential:

- **Consistency:** Everyone knows where to communicate about what, reducing duplicated effort or missed messages.

- **Clarity:** Guidelines prevent vague comments, misplaced updates, or fragmented feedback.

- **Efficiency:** Time is saved when team members don't need to guess where to find the latest discussion or project update.

- **Accountability:** Clear expectations about updates, responsibilities, and responses reduce misunderstandings.

- **Culture:** Communication norms reflect and reinforce a culture of respect, transparency, and shared responsibility.

Let's now break down how to create effective communication norms inside your Asana workspace.

Step 1: Define Your Primary Channels for Communication

Before setting specific rules, align on the **channels** your team will use and their purposes. Within Asana, the main areas where communication happens include:

- **Task comments:** For discussing details directly related to specific tasks.

- **Project messages:** For broader project-level communication or announcements.

- **Team conversations:** For discussions that affect an entire team or multiple projects.

- **Inbox notifications:** For updates and following up on relevant activities.

Norm to establish:

"All task-related discussions must occur in task comments. Avoid using emails or chat tools for discussions about specific Asana tasks to maintain context."

This makes it easy for anyone viewing a task to understand its history and rationale.

Step 2: Standardize Commenting Practices

Task comments are a key element of communication in Asana. Without structure, they can become cluttered or confusing. Here's how to keep them effective:

- **Start with context:** Don't assume the reader remembers everything. Provide brief context.

- **Be concise, but clear:** Avoid long blocks of text. Use bullet points or short paragraphs.

- **Use tagging (@mentions):** Always tag relevant team members to ensure they're notified.

- **Avoid task duplication:** Don't create new tasks when a comment or update will do.

Norm to establish:

"When commenting on tasks, always @mention the assignee or stakeholders, keep messages structured, and summarize the next action if applicable."

Example of a good comment:

@Jordan We've completed user testing. Please review the feedback in the attached document. Let me know if we should revise the wireframes or proceed to development.

Step 3: Define When and How to Use Status Updates

Projects in Asana allow you to post status updates. These are meant for **summarizing progress** and **flagging risks**, not replacing day-to-day communication. However, many teams neglect or misuse this feature.

Best practices for status updates:

- Post them on a **regular schedule** (weekly, bi-weekly, etc.)
- Follow a **consistent format** (e.g., Progress Summary, Upcoming Milestones, Risks/Challenges)
- Link to relevant tasks or milestones
- Keep it high-level, not a task-by-task breakdown

Norm to establish:

"Project leads should post a status update every Friday using our standardized format: Green/Yellow/Red status, summary, blockers, and next steps."

Step 4: Clarify Response Time Expectations

Even in a tool like Asana, some team members may treat comments or updates as optional reading. That leads to delays or missed responsibilities. Set expectations for when responses are needed.

Consider defining:

- **Response time for task comments:** e.g., within 24 hours during workdays
- **Acknowledgment of @mentions or assignments**
- **How to escalate urgent items (e.g., tag + comment + Slack message)**

Norm to establish:

"Team members should acknowledge Asana comments within 1 working day. For urgent issues, escalate by tagging and sending a Slack ping."

This reinforces the importance of maintaining the Asana space as the central source of truth.

Step 5: Encourage Use of Descriptive Task Titles and Details

Communication begins at the point of task creation. Poorly titled tasks can confuse team members and slow things down.

Best practices include:

- Clear, **action-oriented titles** (e.g., "Draft Q3 Campaign Plan" instead of "Marketing Stuff")
- Brief but informative **task descriptions**
- Using **custom fields** to provide structure (e.g., priority level, estimated time)

Norm to establish:

"All new tasks must have a clear, action-based title, a filled-in description, and appropriate custom fields selected."

This prevents the need for back-and-forth clarification later on.

Step 6: Define Meeting vs. Asana Communication

One of the biggest sources of inefficiency is failing to distinguish what should happen in Asana vs. meetings. Many updates and discussions can and **should** be handled asynchronously in Asana to reduce meeting time.

Create norms such as:

- "Weekly stand-ups are Asana-first: updates are posted in project comments before the meeting."
- "Only unresolved blockers or strategic discussions are escalated to a live meeting."

Norm to establish:

"Whenever possible, use Asana for status updates and daily progress sharing. Reserve meetings for collaborative problem-solving or decision-making."

Step 7: Archive Completed Tasks and Clean Up Regularly

Asana can get cluttered with old or irrelevant items. Maintaining a clean workspace is a form of communication—it shows what's active and what's done.

Best practices:

- Use automation rules to move completed tasks to "Done" sections
- Archive completed projects when finished
- Regularly review and close stale tasks

Norm to establish:

"Completed tasks should be marked and moved to the appropriate section. Old or inactive tasks over 30 days will be reviewed and closed during the monthly cleanup."

Step 8: Train and Reinforce Norms

Establishing norms isn't a one-time announcement. You need to **train your team**, **model good behavior**, and **review compliance** periodically.

- Hold onboarding sessions for new members
- Create an internal "Asana Communication Playbook"
- Provide feedback when norms are not followed
- Praise team members who model excellent use of Asana

Norm to establish:

"All new hires must attend an Asana onboarding session and receive our internal Asana Playbook within their first week."

Benefits of Well-Defined Communication Norms

Once established, your team will likely notice immediate benefits:

- Less confusion about responsibilities and deadlines

- Clearer, more actionable updates

- Faster decision-making

- Reduced reliance on meetings and scattered tools

- Higher trust and accountability within the team

As your organization grows, these norms become the foundation for **scalable**, **repeatable**, and **transparent** collaboration practices.

Sample Communication Norms Policy (Summary)

Here's a summarized version of the norms discussed above:

Area	Communication Norm
Task Comments	Use clear structure, @mention relevant people, always add context
Task Creation	Use action-based titles, complete descriptions, and custom fields
Status Updates	Weekly, consistent format, posted by project leads
Response Times	1-day acknowledgment for comments and assignments
Meetings	Use Asana for updates, meetings for discussion
Cleanup	Archive completed tasks, review old items monthly
Onboarding	Train all new hires with a standard Asana playbook

Conclusion: Culture Built Through Communication

Clear communication norms aren't just about using Asana effectively—they're about shaping how your team works together, solves problems, and achieves goals. When everyone understands how to communicate, your projects become faster, more aligned, and more enjoyable to manage.

In the next section, we'll explore how to **stay organized as a team**, including managing workloads, setting priorities, and building systems that scale.

4.3.2 Staying Organized as a Team

Staying organized as a team is both a science and an art. It requires the right combination of tools, systems, culture, and commitment. Asana provides a robust platform to keep every member aligned, accountable, and engaged. But the platform alone isn't enough—teams must actively apply best practices and build habits around clarity, transparency, and collaboration.

This section will explore the principles and actionable strategies teams can use within Asana to maintain a high level of organization, regardless of team size, complexity of projects, or remote/hybrid work models.

Why Team Organization Matters

A disorganized team leads to confusion, missed deadlines, duplicated efforts, and burnout. When people don't know:

- What to do
- Who is responsible
- When it's due
- Why it matters

...it becomes difficult to work effectively. An organized team ensures that:

- Everyone has a clear purpose and role
- Work is visible and trackable
- Collaboration flows smoothly
- Priorities are aligned with goals

Asana acts as a single source of truth, but only if it is structured and used with intention.

II. Establishing a Clear Project Structure

1. Use Consistent Project Templates

Templates save time, promote consistency, and reduce decision fatigue. Teams should create reusable templates for common workflows (e.g., onboarding, marketing campaigns, product launches).

Tips:

- Standardize naming conventions

- Include key sections (e.g., "Planning," "Execution," "Review")

- Preload tasks with owners, deadlines, and dependencies

Templates can be managed in Asana's *Templates* tab or created as a regular project that can be duplicated.

2. Define Clear Ownership and Roles

Every task and subtask in Asana should have an **assignee**—not a group, but a single accountable person. This reinforces clarity and reduces the "someone else will handle it" mentality.

Best Practices:

- Assign a *Project Owner* to manage progress and updates

- Use *Task Collaborators* to involve others without confusion

- Label roles using *Custom Fields* (e.g., "Lead," "Support," "Reviewer")

3. Set Milestones and Priorities

Milestones in Asana highlight major achievements and help track project health. Custom fields can also be used to tag tasks as *High*, *Medium*, or *Low* priority.

How to implement:

- Use **Milestones** for critical phases

- Create **priority fields** and color-code them

- Schedule **weekly reviews** to adjust priorities as needed

III. Organizing Work at the Task Level

1. Break Down Work Clearly

Instead of large, vague tasks, teams should practice **task decomposition**:

- Break goals into actionable items
- Create subtasks for complex deliverables
- Avoid tasks like "Finalize campaign" – instead, break it into "Write copy," "Design assets," "Schedule launch"

This not only clarifies what needs to be done but makes progress measurable.

2. Use Sections, Boards, and Custom Fields

Visual clarity helps teams quickly scan and understand project status. Asana offers several organizational tools:

- **Sections**: Group tasks within projects (e.g., To Do, Doing, Done)
- **Board View**: Ideal for Kanban-style workflows
- **Custom Fields**: Add structured metadata (e.g., priority, status, department)

Example: In a content calendar project, custom fields might include:

- Content Type (Blog, Video, Social)
- Status (Draft, Review, Scheduled)
- Owner Department (Marketing, Design)

3. Maintain Descriptive Task Details

Every task should be self-explanatory:

- Start task names with **verbs** (e.g., "Design homepage banner" vs. "Banner")
- Use the **Description** area to explain what's required
- Attach necessary files and documents
- Use **checklists** or **subtasks** when applicable

IV. Aligning on Communication and Updates

1. Use Comments Strategically

Asana's comment threads help centralize conversations. Avoid switching to email or chat apps unless necessary.

Recommendations:

- Keep conversations task-specific
- Mention team members using *@username*
- Use **comment likes** to acknowledge receipt or agreement

2. Set Up Weekly and Monthly Updates

A cadence of regular updates builds transparency:

- **Weekly Project Updates** (use the *Status* feature in Asana)
- **Monthly Review Projects** with key metrics and discussion threads

Use **status updates** to:

- Summarize current status
- Flag blockers
- Celebrate wins

Encourage feedback and participation from all team members in these updates.

3. Reduce Noise with Notifications Settings

Too many notifications can lead to notification fatigue. Encourage team members to:

- Customize **notification settings** under their profile
- Use the **Inbox** feature in Asana for essential updates
- **Unfollow** tasks or projects they no longer need to monitor

This helps everyone stay informed without being overwhelmed.

V. Encouraging Accountability and Follow-Through

1. Use Due Dates and Deadlines Rigorously

Asana makes it easy to assign due dates. Consistently applying them helps teams:

- Set realistic timelines
- Track progress in **Calendar** and **Timeline** views
- Identify overdue tasks and bottlenecks

Avoid open-ended tasks by always assigning:

- A due date
- An assignee
- A clear description

2. Visualize Workload Across the Team

Use the **Workload view** (in Asana Premium) to prevent burnout and optimize team capacity.

Strategies:

- Balance work across teammates
- Reschedule or redistribute tasks during crunch periods
- Encourage breaks or non-work days in planning

3. Review Progress Regularly

Use **portfolios** or **dashboard widgets** to monitor:

- Task completion rates
- Milestone progress
- Team engagement metrics

Create a shared culture of reflection and improvement by hosting:

- Retrospectives
- End-of-cycle reviews
- Lessons-learned sessions

VI. Building Team Culture Around Asana

A tool is only as effective as the habits behind it. Teams that thrive with Asana make it part of their **team culture**.

1. Embed Asana in Daily Workflows

Encourage team members to:

- Start their day with "My Tasks"
- Check notifications regularly
- Use task comments instead of emails
- Mark tasks complete on time

2. Offer Training and Peer Support

Not everyone learns tools at the same pace. Support each other by:

- Hosting periodic **Asana training sessions**
- Appointing **Asana Champions** to guide adoption
- Creating an internal **knowledge base** of best practices

3. Celebrate Wins Inside Asana

Motivation grows when achievements are recognized. Use:

- Comment threads to praise contributions
- Milestones to mark achievements
- Emojis and gifs to add personality and fun

A healthy team dynamic makes Asana more than a tool—it becomes a collaborative space.

VII. Troubleshooting Common Organizational Challenges

Even organized teams face roadblocks. Here's how to solve them using Asana:

Challenge	Solution in Asana
Overlapping responsibilities	Use Custom Fields to clarify roles
Unclear task status	Standardize labels (e.g., To Do, In Progress)
Too many overdue tasks	Set up recurring review meetings
Low engagement with Asana	Embed usage in onboarding and daily routines
Loss of knowledge over time	Centralize documentation using pinned projects

Conclusion: Organization is a Habit, Not a Destination

Maintaining team organization in Asana is not a one-time setup—it's a continuous process of alignment, review, and adaptation. As teams evolve, so too should the structures and workflows that support them. By following the practices outlined in this chapter, teams can not only stay organized but also thrive in the face of complex, fast-moving work environments.

When your team commits to clarity, ownership, and visibility—and uses Asana as the living system to support that commitment—great things happen.

CHAPTER V
Integrating and Extending Asana

5.1 Connecting Asana with Other Tools

5.1.1 Slack, Zoom, and Microsoft Teams Integrations

Introduction: The Power of Integration

In today's fast-paced, multi-platform work environments, managing communication and collaboration across different tools can be overwhelming. That's where Asana's integration capabilities shine. By connecting Asana with communication platforms like Slack, Zoom, and Microsoft Teams, teams can centralize project conversations, streamline task creation, and reduce the friction of switching between tools.

These integrations allow Asana to function not just as a standalone project management system, but as the command center of your digital workspace—pulling together communication, task management, file sharing, and meeting coordination into one streamlined system.

This section will guide you through how each of these integrations works, what they enable, and how to set them up effectively.

1. Integrating Asana with Slack

Why Integrate Slack with Asana?

Slack is a leading messaging app for teams, and many organizations use it as their primary tool for quick discussions and announcements. However, conversations in Slack can easily get lost in the shuffle. By integrating Slack with Asana, you can:

- Create Asana tasks directly from Slack messages
- Get real-time updates on Asana tasks in Slack channels
- Turn action items in conversations into trackable work
- Minimize app-switching and maintain productivity flow

Key Features of the Integration

- **Create Tasks from Messages**: Highlight a message and use the Asana integration to create a new task. The original message is automatically added to the task description for context.

- **Receive Project Notifications in Slack**: Link an Asana project to a Slack channel to receive notifications about task changes, completions, new assignments, and more.

- **Task Previews**: When you paste an Asana task link in Slack, it expands to show task details like assignee, due date, and status.

- **Smart Suggestions**: Asana can prompt users to turn Slack discussions into tasks using intelligent recommendations.

How to Set It Up

1. Go to your Slack App Directory and search for "Asana".
2. Click **Install**, then authorize your Slack and Asana accounts.
3. Follow the prompts to connect your Asana workspace to specific Slack channels.
4. Use commands like /asana create or /asana link to start managing tasks.

Best Practices for Slack Integration

- **Create a Dedicated #project-updates Channel**: Receive all Asana task updates in one place for easy tracking.

- **Turn Standup Updates into Tasks**: Encourage your team to use message-to-task features during daily check-ins.

- **Avoid Notification Overload**: Only link essential projects to avoid flooding Slack with updates.

---

2. Integrating Asana with Zoom

Why Integrate Zoom with Asana?

Zoom has become the standard for remote meetings, but once a meeting ends, action items can easily be forgotten or misplaced. The Asana + Zoom integration bridges this gap by:

- Allowing you to create Asana tasks directly from Zoom meetings

- Attaching meeting transcripts and recordings to relevant projects

- Enhancing visibility of decisions and follow-ups after meetings

- Providing structure to your meetings through embedded Asana agendas

Key Features of the Integration

- **Asana Meeting Assistant**: Join Zoom meetings with Asana's Meeting Assistant bot, which helps identify key takeaways and convert them into actionable tasks.

- **Meeting Notes and Agendas in Asana**: Plan meetings with shared Asana projects, so all participants are aligned on agenda items and responsibilities.

- **Post-Meeting Follow-Ups**: Automatically create tasks from meeting highlights, assign owners, and set deadlines based on meeting discussions.

How to Set It Up

1. Navigate to the Asana App Directory and search for "Zoom".

2. Click **Add to Asana** and log in with your Zoom credentials.

3. Grant necessary permissions to connect both accounts.

4. Use the integration in project task discussions, or directly within Zoom apps (if supported in your plan).

Best Practices for Zoom Integration

- **Use Asana Projects as Meeting Agendas**: Link relevant project sections to your calendar invites so all topics are covered.

- **Assign Meeting Follow-Ups Immediately**: During meetings, use the integration to assign tasks so that no action item is forgotten.

- **Leverage Asana for Sprint Reviews**: Combine Asana timelines and Zoom for regular progress meetings.

3. Integrating Asana with Microsoft Teams

Why Integrate Microsoft Teams with Asana?

Microsoft Teams is another popular collaboration platform, especially for enterprise and education settings. It combines chat, video, and productivity tools in one environment. Integrating it with Asana means:

- Embedding Asana tasks and projects inside Teams tabs

- Creating new Asana tasks directly within a Teams conversation

- Keeping track of task progress while staying in the Teams interface

- Ensuring accountability during discussions by immediately assigning work

Key Features of the Integration

- **Asana Tabs in Teams Channels**: You can pin an entire Asana project to a channel as a tab, allowing team members to view and interact with it without leaving Teams.

- **Message-to-Task Creation**: Highlight a message in a Teams channel and convert it into an Asana task.

- **Asana Bot Notifications**: Receive task updates and deadline reminders via Teams bots.

- **Meeting Planning with Asana Boards**: Use Asana Kanban boards directly in Teams meetings for structured discussions.

How to Set It Up

1. In Microsoft Teams, go to the **Apps** section and search for "Asana".

2. Click **Add** and sign in with your Asana credentials.

3. Choose which Teams channels or chats you want to link with Asana projects.

4. Add Asana as a tab to relevant channels and authorize necessary permissions.

Best Practices for Microsoft Teams Integration

- **Create a "Work Overview" Tab**: Pin the most important project to the top of each Teams channel for easy access.

- **Assign Work During Team Calls**: Turn live discussion items into tasks during video calls for better follow-through.

- **Use Notifications Wisely**: Customize bot alerts to avoid message fatigue among team members.

4. Choosing the Right Integration for Your Team

Each integration—Slack, Zoom, or Microsoft Teams—has its strengths and best-use cases. Here's a brief comparison to help you choose:

Integration	Best For	Key Strengths
Slack	Fast-moving startups and tech teams	Real-time task creation, lightweight updates
Zoom	Remote and hybrid teams	Meeting-based follow-ups, voice-based workflows
Microsoft Teams	Enterprises and Microsoft 365 users	Deep Office integration, embedded project tabs

You can use more than one integration at a time, especially if your team is spread across platforms. Just be mindful of overlapping notifications and maintain clarity around which tools are used for what.

5. Tips for Maximizing Integration Success

To ensure smooth usage of these integrations:

- **Train Your Team**: Provide onboarding sessions or documentation on how to use integrations effectively.

- **Monitor Usage**: Periodically review how integrations are being used and adjust as needed to reduce noise or overlap.

- **Document Workflows**: Clearly define when and how to use each integration, e.g., "Slack is for daily updates, Asana for task tracking".

- **Regularly Review Permissions**: Especially important in larger organizations to avoid unauthorized access.

Conclusion: Bringing It All Together

Integrating Asana with Slack, Zoom, and Microsoft Teams bridges the gap between conversations and execution. It transforms meetings and messages into measurable actions, ensuring that no important detail falls through the cracks. By leveraging these integrations thoughtfully, you create a powerful ecosystem where communication and productivity coexist seamlessly.

These tools not only save time but also increase accountability and clarity—two of the most vital ingredients in any successful team. When used effectively, Asana becomes the beating heart of your operations, with Slack, Zoom, and Teams acting as its voice, eyes, and ears.

5.1.2 Google Drive, Dropbox, and File Storage Integrations

In a collaborative work environment, sharing files efficiently is essential to productivity. Whether you're developing marketing materials, managing contracts, or building product roadmaps, the ability to connect your project management platform with file storage solutions streamlines the way your team accesses and collaborates on documents. Asana recognizes this need and offers robust integration with popular cloud storage platforms like **Google Drive**, **Dropbox**, **OneDrive**, and others.

This section provides a deep dive into how to integrate these services with Asana, how to make the most of these features, and how to use them in real-world team workflows.

Why File Storage Integrations Matter in Asana

Before diving into the "how-to," it's important to understand the **why**. Integrating file storage tools into Asana provides a range of benefits:

- ☑ **Centralized Collaboration**: Attach relevant files directly to tasks and projects without switching platforms.

- ☑ **Version Control**: Ensure the team is always referring to the most current document version.

- ☑ **Faster Decision Making**: Quickly access supporting documentation, images, reports, or spreadsheets tied to a task.

- ☑ **Reduced Redundancy**: Avoid duplicate uploads and miscommunication from out-of-date attachments.

These integrations help teams work more efficiently, ensuring context is preserved and collaboration remains focused and informed.

1. Integrating Google Drive with Asana

Google Drive is one of the most widely used cloud storage services globally. Asana's integration allows you to connect directly to your Drive account to attach files to any task or comment.

How to Connect Google Drive to Asana

1. **Open a Task** in Asana.

2. Click the **paperclip icon** (📎) or the **attachment section** in the task pane.

3. Choose **"Attach from Google Drive."**

4. A new window will open asking you to log in to your Google account (if not already connected).

5. **Authorize Asana** to access your Google Drive.

6. Once connected, you can **browse folders** or search for the file you want to attach.

Attaching Google Drive Files to Tasks

Once your account is connected:

- You can attach **Docs, Sheets, Slides, PDFs**, and any file stored in Drive.

- Asana will maintain a **live link** to the file, ensuring team members always access the latest version.

- Multiple files can be attached to the same task, and they'll display in the **task pane** for easy access.

Collaborating with Google Drive Files in Asana

Google Drive files maintain their collaboration features even when accessed through Asana:

- You can open the file in Google Drive from within Asana.

- **Comments on the file** in Google Drive remain separate from Asana task comments—but referencing both in context can support richer discussion.

- Changes made in real-time are immediately reflected without needing re-upload.

Use Case Example: Marketing Campaign Planning

Let's say you're running a marketing campaign:

- Each task in your Asana project (e.g., "Write Blog Post", "Design Ad Banner", "Create Landing Page") includes a corresponding **Google Doc** or **Slide deck**.

- Team members assigned to the task can open the document directly from the task pane, add comments or edits, and mark the task complete when done.

- Your project manager doesn't need to chase down assets—they're all centralized and contextually organized.

---

2. Integrating Dropbox with Asana

Dropbox is another cloud storage solution that integrates seamlessly with Asana. Teams who prefer Dropbox often use it for file-heavy projects, especially those involving large media files or proprietary assets.

How to Connect Dropbox to Asana

1. Open the desired task in Asana.

2. Click the **paperclip icon** or go to **"Attach File"**.

3. Select **"Dropbox."**

4. You will be prompted to **log into Dropbox** and **authorize the integration**.

5. Once connected, browse your Dropbox folders and select the desired file.

Using Dropbox in Asana

- Files are embedded as **links**, just like with Google Drive.

- You can preview supported files directly from the task.

- Dropbox allows you to manage **access control** through its own settings (e.g., view-only, edit permissions), which works alongside Asana.

Use Case Example: Creative Agency Workflow

A design agency uses Asana to manage client projects:

- For each client, there's a shared Dropbox folder containing raw design files.

- Tasks such as "Review Logo Draft" or "Send Client Final Files" are linked with relevant Dropbox files.

- Designers and project managers can quickly access assets from the Asana task without opening Dropbox separately.

---

3. Other File Storage Integrations (OneDrive, Box, etc.)

Asana also supports integrations with **Microsoft OneDrive** and **Box**, offering similar functionality. The general process is consistent:

- Navigate to the task.

- Choose "Attach File" and select your storage provider.

- Authenticate and attach the desired file.

These integrations are valuable for organizations that use Microsoft 365 or enterprise file storage solutions.

---

4. Best Practices for Using File Storage with Asana

To maximize efficiency, teams should adopt a few best practices when integrating file storage services with Asana.

Standardize File Naming Conventions

A descriptive file name (e.g., Q2_Sales_Report_FINAL.xlsx instead of report2.xlsx) ensures clarity and minimizes confusion when viewing attachments in a task list.

Link, Don't Upload

Where possible, link to cloud files instead of uploading copies. This ensures everyone always accesses the latest version, and avoids version conflicts or redundant storage usage.

Maintain Folder Organization in Cloud Storage

While Asana links help contextualize files in tasks, maintaining structured folders in Google Drive or Dropbox supports long-term clarity, especially when referencing archived or completed projects.

Limit Access Appropriately

Make sure that shared files have the correct permissions. For example:

- View-only for stakeholders
- Comment-only for external collaborators
- Full edit for the internal team

Proper access control prevents accidental edits or privacy breaches.

Combine with Asana Comments

When linking a file, always add a note in the task comment with the reason for the file or specific instructions (e.g., "Please review slides 3-5 by Friday").

---

5. Troubleshooting and Limitations

File Not Opening?

- Ensure that the user has appropriate access to the file in the external system (e.g., Google Drive permissions).

- If files were moved or deleted from the source platform, links in Asana will break.

File Previews Not Displaying?

- Some file types do not preview natively in Asana but can still be opened in the original application.

Can't Attach Large Files?

- While Asana itself doesn't host the file (only links to them), cloud storage providers may have upload limits. Make sure you're within the storage platform's file size limits.

6. Future-Proofing Your File Management

As remote and hybrid work becomes the norm, centralizing task management and document collaboration is no longer optional—it's essential. Asana's file integration capabilities are continually evolving, with features like:

- Enhanced preview options

- Deeper API-level integration

- AI-powered search across linked documents (e.g., from Google Workspace)

By aligning your team's file management practices with Asana's capabilities, you reduce friction, improve visibility, and boost accountability across your projects.

Summary: Key Takeaways

Practice	Benefit
Use cloud links instead of uploads	Always access the latest file version
Name files clearly	Reduce confusion
Combine attachments with task context	Improve clarity
Maintain permission hygiene	Protect sensitive content

Practice	Benefit
Stay organized in cloud folders	Enable long-term searchability

5.1.3 CRM and Sales Integrations

In today's competitive business landscape, managing customer relationships effectively is more than a strategic advantage—it's a necessity. While Asana excels at task and project management, many teams also rely on Customer Relationship Management (CRM) platforms such as Salesforce, HubSpot, Zoho CRM, and Pipedrive to manage leads, sales pipelines, and client communication. By integrating these CRM tools with Asana, organizations can bridge the gap between sales activities and operational workflows, ensuring that every customer interaction translates into actionable tasks and measurable results.

This chapter explores how to connect CRM and sales tools to Asana, what integrations are available, and how these integrations help streamline processes, reduce manual handoffs, and keep teams aligned around the customer.

1. Why Integrate CRM Tools with Asana?

Bridging Sales and Operations

In many organizations, sales teams operate within CRMs, while delivery, customer success, and project management teams work inside tools like Asana. When these systems are disconnected, important information gets lost in handovers, and accountability becomes blurred. Integrating CRMs with Asana enables a seamless transition from deal closure to execution. For instance, when a deal is marked "Won" in Salesforce, an onboarding project can be automatically created in Asana with predefined tasks, assignees, and deadlines.

Automating Workflows

Manual processes, such as notifying the project team after a new client signs on, assigning onboarding responsibilities, or updating task statuses, are time-consuming and error-prone. Integration automates these processes, ensuring faster turnaround times and fewer dropped balls.

Increasing Visibility and Accountability

With integration, Asana users can view sales context (such as customer deal value, stage, and priority) directly within tasks and projects. Sales and project teams stay informed and accountable without switching between platforms.

2. Popular CRM Integrations with Asana

Several CRM platforms offer built-in or third-party integrations with Asana. Below are the most commonly used CRM tools that work seamlessly with Asana, along with the key capabilities they provide.

Salesforce + Asana

Salesforce, one of the most powerful CRMs in the world, integrates directly with Asana via a native app available in the Salesforce AppExchange and Asana's integrations center.

Key Features:

- Automatically create Asana tasks or projects when opportunities reach certain stages (e.g., "Contract Sent" or "Closed Won").

- Sync Salesforce records to Asana tasks, allowing team members to view and update CRM data directly within Asana.

- Trigger project templates for onboarding, implementation, or customer success tasks.

- Track the lifecycle of a customer—from lead to service delivery—without duplicating data entry.

Use Case Example: When a sales rep marks a deal as "Closed Won" in Salesforce, Asana creates a project titled "Client Onboarding – [Client Name]" using a predefined template that includes tasks like "Welcome email," "Kickoff meeting," "Tech setup," and "Training schedule."

HubSpot + Asana

HubSpot's CRM is widely used by startups and growing companies thanks to its user-friendly interface and free entry-level tier. HubSpot integrates with Asana through tools like Zapier, Automate.io, or native apps from integration providers like Unito.

Key Features:

- Automatically create Asana tasks based on activity in HubSpot (e.g., new lead created, deal stage changed).

- Pass information such as contact name, deal amount, and custom fields into task descriptions.

- Sync task completions back to HubSpot for tracking progress.

Use Case Example: When a marketing-qualified lead (MQL) becomes a sales-qualified lead (SQL) in HubSpot, a new task is created in Asana for the business development rep (BDR) to initiate contact. If the deal progresses, a full client onboarding workflow is triggered.

Pipedrive + Asana

Pipedrive is a CRM designed for salespeople by salespeople, offering clean pipelines and deal tracking. Through Zapier or Integromat (now Make), it integrates easily with Asana.

Key Features:

- Trigger task or project creation in Asana when a deal moves between pipeline stages.

- Assign Asana tasks based on deal owners or priorities in Pipedrive.

- Sync custom data from Pipedrive into Asana task notes or fields.

Use Case Example: When a deal enters the "Proposal Sent" stage in Pipedrive, Asana automatically creates a task for the legal team to review the contract and notifies the account manager.

Zoho CRM + Asana

Zoho CRM is popular among small to medium-sized businesses and offers strong customization. Integration with Asana is possible via Zapier, Zoho Flow, or Unito.

Key Features:

- Task creation based on contact or deal events.

- Push notifications from Asana back into Zoho CRM notes or feeds.

- Automate project templates for recurring sales processes.

3. Integration Methods: Native vs Third-Party

Depending on the CRM you use and your budget or technical expertise, there are different ways to integrate CRM tools with Asana.

Native Integrations

Platforms like Salesforce and HubSpot may offer official Asana apps with robust functionality. These are easier to set up and maintain but may be limited in customization.

Advantages:

- Simple setup

- Support from both platforms

- Reliable sync

Disadvantages:

- Fewer custom workflows

- Often available only in paid tiers

Third-Party Automation Tools

If you need more flexibility or are using a CRM without native support, tools like Zapier, Unito, Make (Integromat), or Automate.io provide customizable triggers and actions between Asana and virtually any CRM.

Examples of Automations:

- When a new deal is created in your CRM, create a matching task in Asana.

- When a task is completed in Asana, update a field in the CRM.

- When a deal closes, trigger a project and assign the onboarding team.

Advantages:

- High customizability

- Works with a wide range of CRMs

- Supports multiple steps and logic

Disadvantages:

- May require some technical setup

- Costs can grow with volume and complexity

4. Best Practices for CRM-Asana Integration

Align Teams on Process Flow

Before connecting systems, map out how leads flow from initial contact to project execution. Make sure both the sales and delivery teams agree on:

- Handoff points
- Required information
- Responsibilities

Use Standardized Project Templates

For predictable sales outcomes like client onboarding or implementation, create standard Asana project templates that are triggered by CRM events. Include:

- Milestones
- Task owners
- Timelines
- Links to key documents

Automate Only What Adds Value

Avoid over-automation. Only automate tasks that improve efficiency and accuracy. For example, creating a new project for every small deal might clutter your Asana workspace.

Monitor and Maintain Integrations

Integration rules and APIs evolve. Regularly test and maintain your connections to ensure they're working correctly. Monitor:

- Task duplication
- Missing data
- Delayed syncs

5. Real-World Example: From Deal to Delivery

Imagine a SaaS company using **Salesforce** for sales and **Asana** for project management. Here's how integration looks in action:

1. **Sales Stage: "Closed Won"**

   o   Sales rep marks deal as won in Salesforce.

2. **Trigger in Asana:**

   o   A new project titled "Client Onboarding – Acme Corp" is created using the onboarding template.

3. **Automatic Task Assignment:**

   o   Tasks like "Set up client account," "Schedule welcome call," and "Send training materials" are assigned to appropriate team members.

4. **Data Visibility:**

   o   Salesforce deal info (deal size, client industry, key contacts) is included in the project description in Asana.

5. **Collaboration Begins:**

   o   The onboarding team starts work immediately, without waiting for a manual handoff or email.

---

6. Final Thoughts

Connecting CRM and sales tools with Asana elevates the efficiency, accuracy, and alignment of your entire organization. By reducing the gap between sales and service delivery, you create a smoother experience for clients and a more collaborative internal culture. Whether you're using native integrations or third-party platforms, the goal remains the same: transform customer success into a repeatable, reliable process—powered by connected tools and empowered people.

5.2 Using Asana Apps and Mobile Versions

5.2.1 Mobile App Overview

Asana is designed to help teams stay organized, productive, and efficient—whether they're working at their desks or on the go. In today's mobile-first world, the ability to manage tasks and projects from anywhere is not a luxury, but a necessity. Asana recognizes this need and offers powerful mobile applications for both iOS and Android platforms that extend the platform's functionality beyond the desktop, enabling users to manage their work on smartphones and tablets.

In this section, we'll explore the features, interface, and best practices for using the Asana mobile app. Whether you're checking off tasks while commuting, communicating with your team during travel, or reviewing a project timeline while attending a meeting, Asana's mobile apps keep you connected and in control.

1. Installing the Asana Mobile App

The Asana mobile app is available for free from the **Apple App Store** (for iOS devices) and the **Google Play Store** (for Android devices). To get started:

1. Open your device's app store.
2. Search for **"Asana: Work in one place"**.
3. Tap **Install** or **Download**.
4. Once installed, open the app and sign in with your existing Asana credentials. If you don't have an account yet, you can create one directly from the app.

The app will prompt you for basic permissions such as access to notifications and file storage (to allow uploading attachments). It's advisable to enable notifications so you're updated on project activities in real-time.

2. Overview of the Mobile Interface

The mobile app's interface is streamlined for clarity and speed, but it retains much of the functionality found in the desktop version.

Home Screen

Upon logging in, the Home screen serves as your dashboard. Here you can:

- See your **Assigned Tasks**.
- Access **Projects** you've recently worked on.
- View **Favorites** (projects or portfolios you've marked for quick access).
- Access the **Inbox** for updates and notifications.

You can quickly search for tasks, projects, teams, or teammates using the search icon at the top-right corner.

Navigation Bar

At the bottom of the screen, you'll find a fixed navigation bar with the following key options:

- **Home** – Your main workspace dashboard.
- **My Tasks** – Tasks assigned to you, sorted by due date or custom sections.
- **Inbox** – Notifications about task changes, mentions, updates, and comments.
- **More (≡)** – Access to projects, teams, settings, and your Asana profile.

---

3. Managing Tasks on Mobile

The mobile app provides a robust task management experience. Here's what you can do:

Creating a New Task

Tap the **+** button (usually found in the corner of the screen) to create a new task. You can:

- Enter a **task name**.
- Add a **description**.
- Set a **due date**.
- Assign the task to yourself or a team member.

- Choose the **project** to which the task belongs.

- Add **subtasks** or attachments.

You can also use **voice input** to dictate task details instead of typing—a useful feature while on the go.

Editing and Updating Tasks

Tap on any task in your list to:

- Change its status (mark complete or incomplete).

- Reassign it.

- Add or remove attachments (photos, files, etc.).

- Leave a comment or mention a teammate.

- Add subtasks to break down work.

- Move the task between sections or projects.

Using the Task Inbox

The **Inbox** tab in the navigation bar acts as your real-time notification center. From here, you can:

- Review comments on tasks.

- See when someone assigns you a task or mentions you.

- Track changes in project status.

- Respond to notifications directly from the app.

Notifications are synchronized across devices, so any action you take on mobile will reflect on desktop and vice versa.

---

4. Project Management on Mobile

Managing entire projects from your mobile device is not only possible—it's intuitive. Though the mobile experience is more compact, you still retain access to all your teams and projects.

Viewing Projects

From the Home screen or the **More** tab, navigate to the **Teams** section to find your projects. Projects are displayed in either:

- **List View** – Displaying tasks in a vertical list.

- **Board View** – Displaying tasks in kanban-style columns.

Tap into a project to:

- Browse tasks grouped by sections or columns.

- View project members and descriptions.

- Add new tasks or update existing ones.

- Use filters to sort by incomplete, overdue, or completed tasks.

Project Timelines and Calendars

Although the mobile app doesn't offer full timeline editing capabilities, you can:

- View the **project calendar**.

- Check **due dates**.

- See project progress indicators (if project tracking is enabled).

For full Gantt-style timeline editing, Asana recommends using the desktop or tablet version.

---

5. Collaboration and Communication on Mobile

Asana's mobile app makes collaboration seamless. You can:

- **Mention teammates** using @username in comments or task descriptions.

- **React to comments** with emojis.

- **Attach files** from your device, cloud storage, or directly from your camera.

- **Join project conversations** through the Messages tab within each project.

Push notifications ensure that you never miss an important update or comment from your team, and you can reply immediately within the app.

6. Offline Access and Syncing

One of the standout features of the Asana mobile app is **offline access**. You can:

- View your tasks and projects.
- Make changes to tasks.
- Leave comments.
- Create new tasks.

Once your device reconnects to the internet, all your offline actions are automatically synced to your Asana account. This makes the app reliable even during travel, remote work in rural areas, or flights without Wi-Fi.

7. Notifications and Custom Settings

You can customize mobile app notifications from your **Profile Settings**. Choose how and when Asana notifies you via:

- Push Notifications
- Email (via account settings)
- Mobile notification preferences per workspace

This level of control ensures you only get notified about what truly matters to you.

8. Tips for Using Asana on Mobile Efficiently

Here are some practical tips to enhance your mobile Asana experience:

- **Use voice-to-text** to quickly create or update tasks when typing isn't convenient.
- **Pin important projects** to your favorites so they're always one tap away.
- **Use widgets** (Android) or **Home Screen shortcuts** (iOS) to access tasks directly.

- **Set aside daily time** to clear your Inbox and My Tasks on mobile to stay organized.
- **Take pictures of whiteboards or notes** and attach them to tasks during meetings.

9. Limitations of the Mobile App

While the mobile app is powerful, it does have limitations:

- Some advanced features (e.g., Portfolio dashboards, custom timeline editing) are restricted or unavailable on mobile.
- Integration management and complex automation setup (Rules, API interactions) are best handled on desktop.
- Bulk editing of tasks and project duplication is limited.

That said, for daily management, updates, and collaboration, the mobile app performs exceptionally well.

10. When to Use Mobile vs. Desktop

Use Case	Mobile App	Desktop App
Quick task updates	✓	✓
Creating simple tasks	✓	✓
Timeline and workload views	✗	✓
Managing integrations	✗	✓
Detailed reporting	✗	✓
Offline work	✓	✗
Team communication	✓	✓

Conclusion

The Asana mobile app is a vital extension of the platform that empowers users to manage tasks and projects from anywhere, anytime. With offline capabilities, smart notifications, and intuitive design, it helps users stay productive and connected even outside the office. While some complex features are reserved for the desktop version, the mobile app offers everything a user needs to keep projects moving forward.

In the next section, we will explore **best practices for using Asana on the go**, along with strategies for maintaining productivity and staying aligned with your team no matter where you are.

5.2.2 Best Practices for Working on the Go

In today's digital and remote-first world, work is no longer confined to an office desk or a single device. Whether you're commuting, working remotely, attending offsite meetings, or simply stepping out for coffee, the ability to stay connected to your work is critical. Asana understands this shift and offers robust mobile solutions to keep you productive wherever you are.

This section explores best practices for **working on the go with Asana's mobile apps**, ensuring that you can maintain clarity, communication, and control over your tasks and projects—anytime, anywhere.

Why Work on the Go with Asana?

Working on the go is not just about being available—it's about **staying efficient and focused** even in a mobile setting. The Asana mobile app is designed to provide a streamlined version of the desktop experience without overwhelming users with clutter or unnecessary options. It allows users to:

- View, update, and complete tasks
- Communicate with team members
- Receive real-time notifications
- Monitor project progress
- Capture ideas and tasks quickly when inspiration strikes

The ability to take action—even briefly—while away from your computer keeps momentum alive and prevents workflow bottlenecks.

Getting the Most Out of the Asana Mobile App

Here are the best practices and strategic tips for using Asana on your phone or tablet effectively:

1. Customize Your Notifications Thoughtfully

The mobile app keeps you updated with push notifications, but too many alerts can become distracting. Balance is key.

Tips:

- **Customize notification settings** to receive only the most important updates—like when you're assigned a task, when a due date is near, or when you're mentioned in a comment.

- Use **"Inbox" filters** to stay focused on what really matters without scrolling endlessly through every update.

Pro Tip: If you work across multiple teams or clients, consider using Asana's **email notifications** for some updates and **mobile push notifications** for critical ones only.

2. Use Voice and Quick Add for Speed

Typing on mobile can be cumbersome, especially when you're on the move. Asana's mobile app includes features like **voice-to-text** and a **Quick Add button** that allows you to rapidly capture thoughts and tasks.

Best Use Cases:

- Dictate a task idea during a commute or after a meeting

- Use Quick Add to create tasks, subtasks, or projects instantly without needing full project context

- Attach a photo or file from your phone to the task for later reference

3. Bookmark or Save Critical Projects for Easy Access

Mobile app navigation is streamlined, but large teams or portfolios can still feel overwhelming. Make use of Asana's **Favorites** feature to pin your most-used projects or tasks for quicker access.

Example:

- Favorite your personal "Today's Tasks" list
- Star your team's Weekly Sprint board
- Save recurring meeting agendas you need to reference often

4. Master Offline Mode

One of Asana's underrated features is its **offline capability**. You can continue to view and even update tasks while offline. Changes will sync automatically once you reconnect to the internet.

Scenarios where this is useful:

- Working on airplanes or trains
- Traveling in remote areas with poor connectivity
- Attending conferences where Wi-Fi is unreliable

Best Practices:

- Open the projects you plan to work on **before going offline** to cache the necessary data
- Add tasks, edit comments, or complete items offline, and let Asana take care of syncing when back online

5. Use Task Prioritization on Mobile

On mobile, it's especially important to stay focused. Use **tags, custom fields**, or Asana's built-in "Today / Upcoming / Later" sorting to prioritize tasks on the go.

How to optimize task prioritization:

- Mark urgent tasks with a priority custom field

- Use colored tags for visual categorization

- Regularly review and clean up your "My Tasks" view to keep it meaningful and current

6. Comment Responsively and Clearly

While you might not write long replies on mobile, you can still **respond to comments**, **mention teammates**, and **acknowledge updates** using quick responses or emojis.

Best Practices:

- Keep comments short and to the point

- Use emojis for fast acknowledgment (👍 = seen, ✅ = done)

- Avoid assigning tasks from comments unless you can clearly articulate the request

7. Use Calendar and Board Views Efficiently

On mobile, **visual task organization** becomes even more valuable. Asana offers **Calendar View** and **Board View** in its mobile app, helping you understand workloads at a glance.

When to use which:

- **Calendar View:** Great for deadlines, due dates, and spotting overloaded days

- **Board View:** Ideal for managing work in stages (e.g., To Do → Doing → Done)

Tip: Rotate your phone to landscape mode for a wider view of Boards or Timelines.

8. Leverage Mobile Widgets (Android and iOS)

Widgets allow you to view tasks, add items, and check your agenda **right from your home screen**—no need to even open the app.

Best Practices:

- Use a widget for your "Today" list

- Add a task from the widget after a phone call or quick idea

- iOS users can place the widget in **StandBy Mode** or **Lock Screen** for quick glance views

9. Review and Reflect During Downtime

Waiting in line? Sitting in an Uber? Use those small windows of time to:

- Review and clean up tasks

- Reassign overdue tasks

- Check in on project progress

- Reply to pending comments

- Set goals or reminders

These small actions add up and help you keep your workspace clean and actionable.

10. Sync Your Calendar App

While not a feature directly in the mobile app, you can **sync Asana tasks with your Google or Outlook Calendar**, making it easier to view Asana deadlines alongside meetings on your phone's calendar.

Benefits:

- No missed due dates

- Better time-blocking and planning

- One unified view of your day or week

Device Optimization Tips

Here are a few more ways to enhance your mobile Asana experience based on the type of device you're using:

For Android Users:

- Enable **dark mode** to save battery and reduce eye strain

- Use **voice commands** via Google Assistant for task creation

- Customize notifications in Android settings for quiet hours

For iOS Users:

- Use **Siri Shortcuts** to automate task actions

- Add tasks through the **Share Sheet** from Safari or email

- Leverage **Focus Mode** with specific Asana notifications allowed

---

Common Pitfalls to Avoid When Working Mobile-First

- **Avoid over-delegating or making critical changes from mobile** without full project context

- **Don't rely solely on mobile** for long-term planning or high-level reporting—it's better for execution and quick actions

- **Keep comments professional and clear**, even when typed quickly

- **Watch out for duplicate tasks**, especially when adding new items while multitasking

---

The Future of Mobile Work in Asana

As remote and hybrid work continue to grow, Asana is consistently updating its mobile offerings. Expect improvements in:

- AI-based task suggestions

- More robust mobile reporting

- In-app video summaries and meeting notes integration

- Location-based task suggestions or geotagged inputs

Keeping your mobile app updated ensures you benefit from these features as they're rolled out.

Final Thoughts: Embrace Asana Wherever You Are

The goal of mobile work is **flexibility without compromise**. With Asana's mobile app, you're empowered to stay organized, communicate clearly, and move work forward no matter where you are. By applying the best practices above, you'll strike the perfect balance between responsiveness and efficiency—without falling into the trap of being "always on."

Take a moment now to:

- Customize your mobile settings

- Set up key widgets or shortcuts

- Define your "on-the-go" work routine

The next time you're away from your desk, Asana will be right there in your pocket, ready to help you build and maintain your perfect workflow.

5.3 Extending Asana Capabilities

5.3.1 Using Zapier for Advanced Automation

In today's fast-paced work environments, repetitive manual tasks can drain valuable time and resources. This is where automation tools like **Zapier** come in. Zapier allows you to connect Asana with thousands of other web apps, enabling you to automate workflows without writing a single line of code. Whether you want to create tasks in Asana from emails, calendar events, or form submissions, Zapier can help you do it—all automatically.

In this section, you'll learn how Zapier works, how it connects with Asana, and how to build powerful automations ("Zaps") that enhance productivity and reduce friction in your workflows.

What is Zapier?

Zapier is a no-code automation platform that connects over **6,000+ apps**, allowing users to create workflows between tools they use every day. Each **Zap** (Zapier's term for an automated workflow) consists of a **trigger** and one or more **actions**.

For example:

- **Trigger**: A new row is added to a Google Sheet
- **Action**: Create a new task in Asana

By setting up Zaps, you eliminate the need for manual data entry, avoid communication silos, and create seamless interactions between your favorite apps and Asana.

Why Use Zapier with Asana?

Here are a few compelling reasons to consider Zapier for your Asana setup:

- **Cross-Platform Integration**: Connect Asana to apps like Gmail, Slack, Google Forms, Trello, Salesforce, Typeform, Calendly, and thousands more.
- **Time-Saving Automation**: Eliminate repetitive tasks such as manually copying tasks from emails or moving information across platforms.

- **Custom Workflows**: Tailor automations to your unique business processes, including conditional logic and multi-step workflows.

- **No Coding Required**: Zapier's intuitive interface is accessible to non-technical users while still offering power and flexibility.

Getting Started with Zapier and Asana

To begin using Zapier with Asana, follow these steps:

1. Create a Zapier Account

- Visit zapier.com and sign up for a free or paid plan.

- Free plans allow you to create single-step Zaps, while premium plans unlock multi-step workflows, filters, paths, and more.

2. Connect Your Asana Account

- In Zapier, go to "My Apps" and search for "Asana."

- Click "Connect" and log into your Asana account using OAuth authorization.

- Choose the Asana workspace and grant permissions.

3. Explore Popular Asana Zaps

Here are a few pre-built Zaps available in the Zapier directory:

- Create Asana tasks from new Gmail messages

- Add Asana tasks for new Google Calendar events

- Turn Typeform responses into Asana tasks

- Post new Asana tasks to a Slack channel

You can browse templates or start from scratch to build a custom Zap.

Building Your First Zap with Asana

Let's walk through an example of creating a Zap that automatically creates a task in Asana when a new row is added in a Google Sheet.

Step-by-Step Guide: Google Sheets to Asana Task

Step 1: Set the Trigger

- **App**: Google Sheets
- **Event**: New Spreadsheet Row
- **Account**: Connect your Google account
- **Spreadsheet**: Choose your file
- **Worksheet**: Select the sheet where the data is being added

Step 2: Set the Action

- **App**: Asana
- **Event**: Create Task
- **Account**: Choose your Asana account
- **Workspace**: Select your workspace
- **Project**: Choose the project where tasks should be created
- **Task Name**: Map it from a cell in the spreadsheet
- **Due Date, Description, Assignee, etc.**: Optional fields you can customize

Step 3: Test and Publish

- Zapier allows you to test the Zap before turning it on.
- Once confirmed, click **"Publish Zap"** and let automation do the rest.

Multi-Step Zaps for Advanced Users

Multi-step Zaps allow you to go beyond basic automation by chaining several actions together. For example:

Scenario: Capture a Typeform Survey and Turn It into a Full Task Package

1. **Trigger**: Typeform submission
2. **Action 1**: Create a task in Asana

3. **Action 2**: Add subtasks to the main task

4. **Action 3**: Send a Slack message to notify the team

5. **Action 4**: Update a Google Sheet for tracking

Multi-step Zaps are ideal for complex processes such as onboarding new clients, managing support tickets, or launching new campaigns.

Using Filters, Delays, and Paths in Zaps

Zapier offers powerful tools to refine and customize your workflows:

Filters

Run a Zap only if specific conditions are met. Example: Only create a task if a form response includes "urgent."

Delays

Add a delay between steps. Example: Wait 24 hours before assigning a follow-up task.

Paths

Create conditional workflows based on responses or triggers. Example: If the email contains "invoice," route it to the finance team; otherwise, assign it to the general queue.

These features make your automations smarter and more aligned with business logic.

Best Practices for Using Zapier with Asana

1. Start Simple

Begin with single-step Zaps to understand how data flows. Gradually add complexity as your confidence grows.

2. Organize Your Zaps

Name your Zaps clearly, and group them by function or department to stay organized, especially in larger teams.

3. Use Custom Fields in Asana

Zapier can map data to custom fields, allowing greater structure in task organization and filtering within Asana.

4. Monitor Performance

Regularly check your task history in Zapier to ensure workflows are functioning properly and identify any errors.

5. Collaborate with Your Team

Work with other team members to understand what processes could be automated. Zapier works best when it's part of a larger workflow optimization effort.

Common Use Cases by Department

Marketing

- Turn new Facebook Lead Ads into Asana tasks
- Schedule Asana content tasks from Google Calendar events

Sales

- Log CRM deals in Asana for fulfillment workflows
- Create tasks from new rows in HubSpot or Salesforce

Operations

- Trigger task templates when onboarding new vendors
- Automate reminders based on recurring tasks

Customer Support

- Create Asana tasks from Intercom or Zendesk tickets
- Route support issues to appropriate teams automatically

Limitations and Considerations

While Zapier is powerful, it's not perfect for every scenario. Consider the following:

- **Rate Limits**: Zapier and Asana both have rate limits. Heavy automation may hit these.

- **Real-Time Processing**: Some Zaps have slight delays (minutes, not seconds).

- **Complex Data Handling**: Very intricate business logic might require custom scripting or a developer-driven solution.

In such cases, using **Asana's API** directly or hiring a developer to build a more robust integration may be more effective.

When to Use Native Asana Automation vs. Zapier

Asana itself offers **Rules**, a built-in automation system for internal processes. So when should you use Zapier instead?

Use Case	Asana Rules	Zapier
Inside Asana only	☑	⊘
Involving external tools	⊘	☑
Multi-app, complex logic	⊘	☑
Simple field updates	☑	⊘
Requires code or custom steps	⊘	☑ (via Webhooks or Code by Zapier)

Use **Asana Rules** for internal consistency, and **Zapier** when your automation crosses into other platforms.

Summary and Next Steps

Zapier opens the door to a world of powerful automations that supercharge your Asana workflows. From simple task creation based on emails to advanced, multi-step operations involving multiple platforms, Zapier acts as a bridge between your tools, your team, and your goals.

To get started:

1. Identify repetitive tasks in your Asana use.

2. Explore available Zaps or create your own.

3. Start small, then build more advanced workflows.

4. Review and maintain your Zaps regularly.

With the right automation in place, you'll free up time, reduce errors, and empower your team to focus on what really matters: creating value and delivering results.

5.3.2 Exploring API and Developer Options

Asana is not just a powerful task and project management platform—it's also an extensible ecosystem. While its out-of-the-box features cover a wide range of team collaboration needs, organizations with specific workflows or complex systems can benefit from extending Asana using its **Application Programming Interface (API)** and developer tools. This section delves into what the Asana API offers, how developers can build custom solutions on top of Asana, and real-world use cases where extending Asana creates significant value.

Understanding the Asana API

The Asana API is a **RESTful web service** that allows developers to access and manipulate nearly every element of Asana programmatically. This includes tasks, projects, users, teams, custom fields, attachments, comments, portfolios, goals, and more.

Key Features of the Asana API

- **Full access to core objects** like tasks, projects, workspaces, and teams.

- **Webhooks** for real-time event notifications (e.g., when a task is created or completed).

- **OAuth 2.0** support for secure authorization and user access.

- **Pagination and rate limits** for efficient, scalable usage.

- **Support for custom fields and forms**, allowing more personalized workflows.

The API is accessible via simple HTTP requests, and responses are returned in **JSON format**, which makes it easy to use with any modern programming language, especially JavaScript, Python, or Ruby.

When to Use the Asana API

You might consider using the API in the following scenarios:

- **Automating repetitive tasks** (e.g., creating tasks from a form submission).

- **Building internal dashboards** that aggregate Asana data with other business intelligence sources.

- **Syncing Asana with other software tools**, such as CRMs, finance systems, or custom ERP platforms.

- **Customizing workflows** for specific industries or teams.

- **Embedding task creation or status updates** into customer-facing apps or intranets.

Getting Started with the Asana API

1. Setting Up a Developer App

To begin, you need to register an app on the Asana Developer Console. (https://app.asana.com/0/my-apps) This app will provide:

- A **client ID** and **client secret** for OAuth authentication.

- A place to define your **redirect URIs**.

- A sandbox to test API usage and manage scopes.

If you're building internal tools (not for public distribution), you can use **personal access tokens (PATs)** instead of setting up OAuth. These tokens are easier for personal use and testing.

Tip: Never expose personal access tokens or client secrets in your frontend code. Always use them securely in a backend environment.

---

2. Making Your First API Call

A simple example in **Python** using the popular requests library:

```
import requests

headers = {

    "Authorization": "Bearer <your_personal_access_token>"

}

response = requests.get("https://app.asana.com/api/1.0/projects", headers=headers)

print(response.json())
```

This code fetches all projects visible to the user. From here, you can use endpoints like:

- GET /tasks
- POST /tasks
- PUT /tasks/{task_gid}
- GET /projects/{project_gid}/tasks
- And many more...

3. Understanding Object Relationships

Asana has a **graph-style architecture**, where objects are connected in a hierarchical and relational structure:

- A **workspace or organization** contains multiple **teams**.

- Teams contain **projects**.

- Projects contain **tasks**.

- Tasks can have **subtasks**, **attachments**, and **comments**.

This structure means developers can navigate the entire workspace programmatically using API endpoints.

Using Webhooks for Real-Time Updates

Webhooks allow your app to receive updates from Asana in **real time**. Instead of polling the API constantly, you can set a webhook to notify your app when something changes.

For example, set a webhook to monitor a project. Whenever a task is added or completed, your app can trigger an action—like sending a Slack message, updating a CRM field, or notifying a stakeholder.

Important: Your app must provide a publicly accessible HTTPS endpoint for webhook validation and event delivery.

OAuth vs. Personal Access Tokens

Feature	OAuth	Personal Access Token (PAT)
Best for	Multi-user/public apps	Single-user or internal tools
Security	More secure (token rotation)	Less secure if leaked
Scopes	Granular access control	Full access

Feature	OAuth	Personal Access Token (PAT)
Recommended use	Production apps	Testing and internal tools

Use **OAuth** for anything that scales beyond your personal workspace or needs to be distributed.

Advanced Use Cases

1. Building a Custom Client Dashboard

Imagine your company offers digital marketing services. Each client project lives in Asana, and you want to offer clients a branded portal to:

- View their project status

- See completed and pending tasks

- Upload files or ask questions

Using the API, you can:

- Pull project data and render it in a custom dashboard.

- Enable file uploads that post directly into an Asana task.

- Display project progress using portfolio metrics.

2. Automating Onboarding Workflows

Your HR department uses Asana to onboard new hires. You can build a script that:

- Creates a new project from a template

- Assigns tasks to different departments

- Adds due dates based on the hire date

- Sends Slack notifications to relevant team leads

This entire flow can be triggered automatically through the Asana API when a new hire is entered in your HR system.

3. Connecting to Internal BI Tools

Export Asana data into a data warehouse and feed it into dashboards built with tools like Tableau, Power BI, or Looker. You can analyze:

- Task completion trends

- Bottlenecks by team

- Cycle time per project

Use Asana's API to extract and normalize the data, then transform it for analytics.

Developer Resources and Tools

Asana provides robust resources for developers:

- **API Reference**: https://developers.asana.com/docs

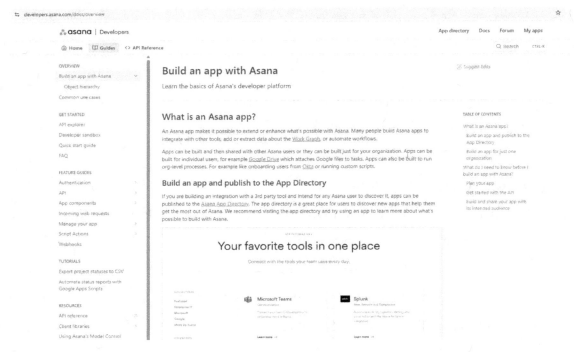

- **Developer Console**: Register and manage apps

- **Open-Source SDKs**:

    o Asana Node.js SDK (https://github.com/Asana/node-asana)

o Python SDK (https://github.com/Asana/python-asana)

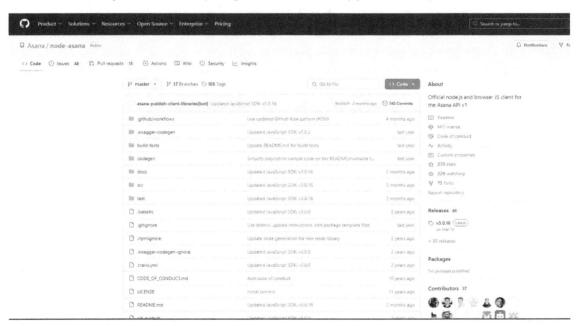

- **Community and Support**:

    ○   GitHub Issues and Feature Requests

Security and Best Practices

- **Rate Limits**: Asana enforces rate limits to protect system stability. Always monitor headers like X-RateLimit-Remaining to avoid being throttled.

- **Error Handling**: Build robust error handling for cases like 429 Too Many Requests, 403 Forbidden, or 401 Unauthorized.

- **Data Protection**: Encrypt sensitive data and never store access tokens in public repos.

- **Modular Code Design**: Abstract API interactions into reusable modules to reduce code duplication and increase scalability.

- **Respect User Consent**: With OAuth apps, always be transparent about the data you access and provide a way to revoke access.

What You Can't Do with the API (Yet)

Asana's API is powerful but not limitless. Some limitations include:

- No real-time task editing (you still need to make update calls).

- Limited access to audit logs or historical versioning.

- No access to certain premium-only features unless the authenticated user has permission.

Conclusion: Why the API Matters

The Asana API opens a world of opportunity for teams looking to tailor their workflows to match unique operational needs. Whether you're integrating Asana with an internal system, automating repetitive tasks, or creating custom dashboards, the developer tools offered by Asana are powerful and flexible.

In today's collaborative world, tools like Asana are no longer isolated platforms—they are **living systems** that can be extended, customized, and embedded into every aspect of work.

By learning to use the API and understanding its potential, you equip your organization with **supercharged project management capabilities** that go beyond the ordinary. And most importantly, you help your team focus on what matters most: **getting meaningful work done**.

Conclusion

Reflecting on Your Workflow Journey

As you reach the end of *Asana Step-by-Step: Build Your Perfect Workflow*, it's the perfect time to pause, look back at what you've accomplished, and chart the path forward. Whether you began this book as a complete beginner or as someone already familiar with the basics of Asana, you've now gained a comprehensive understanding of how to manage your work, your team, and your time using this powerful tool.

But beyond mastering the technical features, this journey has likely changed *how* you think about work: how it flows, how it gets done, and how it can be improved. Asana isn't just a tool—it's a mindset. It's a framework for clarity, alignment, and accountability. In this final section, we'll explore the key reflections from your learning journey, encourage you to assess how far you've come, and offer some guidance on how to continue growing with Asana well into the future.

1. Looking Back: What You've Learned

Over the chapters of this guide, you've built a foundation in Asana that goes beyond surface-level usage. You now understand:

The Basics of Asana

- How to create and manage tasks, assign them to team members, and set due dates
- How to use different project views (List, Board, Calendar, Timeline)
- How to structure projects with sections, tags, and custom fields

Managing Complex Projects

- Building workflows with dependencies and milestones
- Monitoring project progress with dashboards and reporting tools
- Automating repetitive processes with rules and templates

Collaborating with Teams

- Effective communication through comments, mentions, and conversations
- File sharing and centralized documentation
- Coordinating team efforts with workload management and performance tracking

Extending Asana's Power

- Integrating third-party apps like Slack, Google Drive, and Zoom
- Working on the go with mobile apps and browser extensions
- Leveraging advanced automation tools like Zapier and Asana's API

Each of these skills contributes not only to your productivity but also to your ability to manage teams, scale processes, and drive results with confidence and clarity.

---

2. Reflecting on Your Growth

Now that you've come this far, it's valuable to take a moment to reflect on your personal or organizational transformation. Consider the following questions as a guided reflection:

How Has Your Workflow Improved?

- Are you spending less time in status meetings?
- Is your team more aligned on project goals and timelines?
- Have you reduced task duplication, missed deadlines, or confusion?

What Bottlenecks Have You Resolved?

- Were you able to streamline intake processes with forms?
- Did automation reduce manual follow-ups?
- Are priorities clearer across the team?

What Still Needs Optimization?

- Are there tasks or processes that feel messy or hard to track?
- Are team members fully engaged in using Asana, or is adoption still inconsistent?

- Have you reviewed your workflows recently for improvement opportunities?

Reflection is not about perfection—it's about awareness. Knowing where you stand is the first step in deciding where to go next.

---

3. Developing a Continuous Improvement Mindset

The true value of any work management platform lies not in the initial setup, but in its evolution. The more you use Asana, the more insight you gain into how your team works best. Here are strategies to maintain momentum and continue growing:

Run Regular Workflow Reviews

Set aside time every quarter to review your major projects and workflows:

- What's working?
- What's outdated?
- What could be automated?

Involve your team in these reviews so that improvements are grounded in real user feedback.

Foster a Culture of Ownership

Asana works best when everyone feels empowered to use it. Encourage your team to:

- Keep tasks and projects updated
- Proactively communicate in Asana instead of siloed tools
- Suggest improvements or new rules/automations

Make Training a Habit

Onboard new team members thoroughly and regularly update your team on new Asana features. You might:

- Create short Loom videos showing internal workflows
- Host "Asana Tips & Tricks" sessions
- Share best practice documents or help center articles

4. Adapting Asana as Your Organization Grows

Asana is scalable—what works for a 5-person team can evolve into something fit for a 500-person company. But growth comes with complexity. Here's how to adapt:

Moving to Portfolios and Goals

As your projects multiply, consider using **Portfolios** to group related efforts and monitor their health. **Goals** help you align daily work to quarterly or annual objectives.

Using Advanced Reporting

Use **Universal Reporting** to track trends across projects:

- How many tasks were completed last quarter?

- What's the average time to completion?

- Which teams are over/under capacity?

Creating Department-Wide Standards

To ensure consistent quality, develop templates for repeatable projects:

- Marketing campaign templates

- Product development checklists

- Customer onboarding workflows

Standardization frees up mental energy and reduces errors.

5. Common Pitfalls and How to Avoid Them

Even with the best intentions, it's easy to fall into certain traps. Here are common issues and how to prevent them:

Overcomplicating Your Setup

Too many custom fields, rules, or sections can lead to user fatigue. Keep your system as simple as possible—and no simpler.

Relying on Asana Alone for Communication

While Asana is excellent for task-based communication, don't forget the importance of real-time conversation. Use meetings or chat tools for nuanced discussions and decision-making.

Failing to Maintain Projects

Old, incomplete, or abandoned projects clutter your workspace and reduce trust in the system. Archive what you don't use and keep your workspace clean.

---

6. The Human Side of Workflow

Tools like Asana are only as good as the people using them. The most efficient workflow is still vulnerable to burnout, lack of clarity, or poor team morale. To build truly effective teams, focus on:

Psychological Safety

Encourage team members to voice concerns, propose changes, and admit when something isn't working. Great workflows come from honest feedback.

Recognition and Transparency

Use Asana to publicly recognize contributions, log achievements, and celebrate milestones.

Balancing Workload and Wellbeing

Workload management tools are not just for tracking—they're for protecting team health. Avoid over-assigning, and use Asana as a conversation starter about capacity.

---

7. Staying Updated with Asana's Evolution

Asana continues to roll out new features and improvements. Stay up-to-date by:

- Joining the Asana Community Forum https://forum.asana.com/

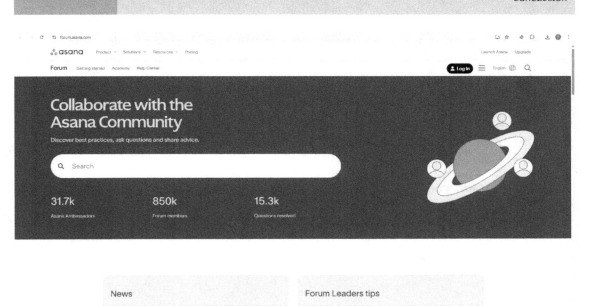

- Reviewing product updates in the "What's New" tab within the platform

Make it a habit to explore what's new each quarter—and reassess how new features can improve your workflows.

8. Your Next Steps

Now that you've completed this book, here's how you can keep your momentum:

- **Implement what you've learned.** Start small—refine one process or one team's workflow.
- **Teach someone else.** The best way to deepen your understanding is to share it.
- **Commit to iteration.** No system is ever final. Work evolves, and so should your setup.
- **Celebrate your wins.** Take note of how far you've come. Productivity is progress, and progress is worth celebrating.

Final Thoughts

You've just completed a comprehensive journey through Asana's tools, features, and philosophies. But more importantly, you've developed the mindset of someone who doesn't just do work—but designs it intentionally.

Asana is more than task tracking. It's about building systems that help people do their best work, together. Whether you're managing a small creative project or steering a large product launch, your ability to shape that journey—clearly, collaboratively, and with confidence—is now in your hands.

So go ahead: **Build your perfect workflow.** You've got the tools, the knowledge, and the vision to make it happen.

Tips for Continuous Improvement

Asana is not just a tool you learn once and forget—it's a dynamic, evolving platform that can grow with your team, your projects, and your organization. By the time you've reached this final chapter, you've gained a thorough understanding of how to navigate the Asana interface, manage projects and tasks, collaborate with teammates, automate workflows, and integrate external tools. However, the real magic of Asana lies in **continuous improvement**—the ongoing refinement of how you work.

This section will guide you through proven strategies, real-world practices, and mindset shifts to help you **continuously improve your workflows, team collaboration, and project outcomes** using Asana. Whether you are a solo user, a team lead, or a department manager, these tips will ensure that your work management processes stay aligned with your goals, scale as your workload increases, and evolve as your team matures.

1. Regularly Review and Refine Workflows

Just like a garden needs regular care to thrive, your workflows in Asana require periodic reviews and adjustments to remain efficient and aligned with your business needs.

Conduct Monthly Workflow Audits

Set a recurring reminder in Asana to audit your projects monthly. During the audit, ask:

- Are any tasks consistently delayed?

- Are projects cluttered or difficult to navigate?

- Are the custom fields and tags still relevant?

- Are we using the right project view (List, Board, Calendar, Timeline)?

Use the answers to these questions to make informed adjustments that reduce friction and improve clarity.

Incorporate Feedback Loops

Encourage your team to provide feedback on how they're using Asana. Use comment threads or forms to collect suggestions. This can reveal:

- Bottlenecks in task approvals

- Confusion around project structure

- Suggestions for new automations or integrations

Feedback is one of the most powerful tools for continuous improvement.

2. Evolve Your Use of Features

You may have started with the basics—tasks, assignees, and due dates—but Asana offers a wide variety of advanced features that can elevate your productivity.

Adopt Advanced Automations

Gradually introduce more complex rules, such as:

- Auto-assigning tasks when moved into specific columns

- Triggering alerts when due dates are missed

- Marking subtasks as dependent on parent tasks

Automations reduce the mental load of micromanaging repetitive work and allow your team to focus on what truly matters.

Use Portfolios and Goals for Higher-Level Planning

If you manage multiple projects, use **Portfolios** to group them and track overall progress. Combine this with **Goals** to link your tasks and projects to broader strategic objectives. This creates visibility and alignment across teams and initiatives.

Explore Custom Templates

Instead of creating projects from scratch, save time by creating **custom templates** for repetitive workflows such as:

- Onboarding new hires

- Launching marketing campaigns
- Managing product sprints

Templates ensure consistency, reduce errors, and speed up project kickoffs.

---

3. Upskill Your Team

The most powerful tool in your productivity toolbox is a well-trained team. Continuous improvement includes **investing in people**, not just platforms.

Offer Role-Based Training

Asana is used differently by different roles. Tailor your training efforts accordingly:

- Team leads: focus on reporting, dashboards, and workload
- Project managers: dive into dependencies and milestones
- Individual contributors: optimize for task management and daily planning

Use Asana Academy, webinars, and internal documentation to train efficiently.

Promote Peer Learning

Encourage team members to share:

- Time-saving shortcuts or views
- New use cases they've discovered
- Favorite integrations

This creates a culture of shared growth and collaborative learning.

Celebrate Asana Champions

Identify and empower "Asana Champions" within each department—team members who are enthusiastic and skilled at using Asana. They can:

- Offer on-the-spot support to peers
- Help onboard new team members

- Act as the bridge between teams and admin users

---

4. Standardize and Document Best Practices

Consistency is key for scaling effective use of Asana. As your organization matures, create internal documentation that outlines **how your team uses Asana**.

Create an Internal Asana Playbook

This playbook can include:

- Naming conventions for tasks and projects
- Guidelines on when to use subtasks vs. tasks
- When and how to use comments, tags, and custom fields
- Rules for setting deadlines and priorities

Having a shared playbook minimizes confusion and ensures everyone is working the same way.

Use Templates for Process Standardization

Templates are not only for speed—they're also for **standardization**. Use them to embed your best practices into repeatable workflows. For example:

- Use required custom fields in templates to ensure key information is always filled out
- Include pre-written task descriptions and checklists
- Pre-assign roles or steps in multi-person workflows

---

5. Measure What Matters

Continuous improvement is only possible if you track your progress. Asana provides several tools to help you **measure efficiency, output, and engagement**.

Use Dashboards and Reporting Widgets

Create dashboards for teams, projects, or portfolios. Use widgets to monitor:

- Completed tasks per assignee
- Overdue tasks
- Time to completion

These insights help identify bottlenecks and celebrate high-performing teams.

Review Goals and OKRs

If your team sets Objectives and Key Results (OKRs), align them with Asana Goals. Review them regularly to ensure progress is on track and team efforts are aligned with business priorities.

Analyze Workload Data

For managers, **Workload View** provides a visual representation of team capacity. Use it to:

- Prevent burnout
- Reallocate tasks efficiently
- Identify over- or under-utilized team members

6. Stay Informed and Future-Proofed

Asana continuously adds new features, improvements, and integrations. Staying informed ensures you can adapt and take advantage of these tools for better outcomes.

Participate in the Asana Community

Join the Asana Community Forums to:

- Ask questions and solve problems
- Learn how other teams are using Asana
- Suggest product ideas and give feedback

It's a great place to grow your expertise and build connections with other productivity enthusiasts.

Test New Features in Sandbox Projects

If your team is large or your workflows are complex, consider testing new processes or features in a sandbox project before rolling them out organization-wide.

---

7. Build a Culture of Improvement

Technology alone cannot create productivity. The human element—**your culture**—must be aligned with a mindset of growth and adaptability.

Encourage Openness to Change

Asana workflows will inevitably need to evolve. Foster a team culture where change is welcomed, not resisted. Regularly communicate:

- Why changes are being made
- How they will improve outcomes
- What support is available for learning

Recognize and Reward Innovation

If a team member finds a better way to use Asana, acknowledge and share it. Small improvements can lead to major efficiencies over time.

Practice Regular Retrospectives

Hold monthly or quarterly retrospectives to reflect on how your team is using Asana. Use questions like:

- What's working well?
- What could be improved?
- What should we stop doing?

Turn the insights from these discussions into action steps for evolving your workflows.

Final Thoughts

Continuous improvement in Asana isn't about doing more for the sake of it. It's about working smarter, being intentional, and enabling your team to focus on meaningful work. With the right mindset, regular reviews, and a commitment to growth, you can transform Asana from a task manager into a **strategic driver of success**.

This book has equipped you with the knowledge to **get started**, **optimize**, and **scale** your use of Asana. From here on, the journey is yours to shape—one improvement at a time.

Acknowledgments

To our readers,

Thank you.

Thank you for choosing this book and investing your time in learning how to master Asana. Whether you are a beginner just starting out or an experienced user looking to refine your workflow, your commitment to personal and professional growth is truly inspiring.

Writing this guide has been a journey rooted in one goal: to help individuals and teams work smarter, not harder. We are honored that you've allowed this book to be a part of your journey toward building better systems, improving collaboration, and achieving your goals.

We hope this guide has empowered you to use Asana with confidence and clarity—and that it continues to serve as a valuable reference as you build your perfect workflow.

If this book helped you, please consider recommending it to a friend, colleague, or fellow professional. Your support not only helps others benefit from it but also allows us to keep creating practical, actionable guides like this one.

Above all, we're grateful that you're out there doing the work—one task, one project, and one collaboration at a time. Keep building. Keep learning. Keep going.

With gratitude,